I.S.A.M. Monographs: Number 22

Jerome Kern
in Edwardian London

ANDREW LAMB

I.S.A.M. Monographs: Number 22

Jerome Kern in Edwardian London

ANDREW LAMB

Institute for Studies in American Music
Conservatory of Music
Brooklyn College
of the City University of New York

To my grandfather,
John Lamb,
who recalls seeing
"How'd You Like to Spoon with Me?"
staged in Edwardian England

CONTENTS

PREFACE

In recent years books on American popular song have provided an increasingly detailed and well documented coverage of the careers, output, and private lives of the major exponents of the genre. During 1980 a particularly significant gap in the coverage was filled with a remarkably detailed book by Gerald Bordman on the man widely accepted as the founding father of American popular theater song—Jerome Kern.[1]

The documentary sources that Bordman assembled with remarkable singlemindedness and persistence not only added much detail to our previous knowledge about Kern but also corrected many earlier inaccuracies. This is true not least of one area that often represents a difficult one for American researchers and writers, namely the involvement of many American musical-comedy songwriters with the London theater. For Kern especially this is important because of his substantial early involvement with London, which provided a basis not only for his own future development but indeed for the conquest of the London stage by American musicals. Moreover, Kern's early visits to London had especial personal significance in that it was in England in 1910 that he married an English girl.

All of this Bordman has chronicled in far greater detail and with far greater accuracy than any previous writer. Yet ironically it is the very detail into which Bordman enters that highlights shortcomings in his coverage. The aim of the present study is to consider in further detail Kern's involvement with the England of Edward VII—a period that ended when Kern returned home with his English bride late in 1910.

It is in the very nature of this study that it should contain quite a number of corrections to Bordman's Kern biography. Yet this should not be taken as a denigration of Bordman's efforts. The author understands full well the phenomenal dedication that must have gone into Bordman's book, and wishes to express first of all a huge debt of admiration and gratitude to him. Although the research behind this study began long before Bordman's book appeared, it would never have been developed to its present scale without the stimulus of the information that Bordman assembled.

In compiling the study, I have had recourse to such standard British theatrical sources as *The Green Room Book* and its successor *Who's Who in the Theatre*, to *Who's Who* and *The Post Office London Street Guide*, to the files of *The Times*, *The Era*, *The Stage*, and *The Play Pictorial*, and to the various books of Raymond Mander and Joe Mitchenson, which are mines of information on the London theater. Citations of other books used will be found among the notes. For permission to use copyrighted material I am grateful to Hutchinson Publishing for the excerpts from the autobiography of George Grossmith, and to Dean Kay of T. B. Harms Company for the illustration from Kern's "The Gay Lothario."

For help of various kinds I owe warm thanks particularly to the following: James J. Fuld of New York for copyright dates of Kern's compositions from Library of Congress records, and for information derived from his remarkable collection of sheet music; Kurt Gänzl, who read my typescript and permitted me access to his forthcoming monumental *The British Musical Theatre*, thereby bringing to my attention instances that I would otherwise have missed of Kern's songs being used in London shows; John M. Garrett of Chappell International for access to the archives of Hopwood & Crew; Harry Shaberman of EMI Music for access to the sheet-music files of Francis, Day & Hunter; the staff of the British Library and the Performing Right Society; the Borough Librarians of High Wycombe, and the London Borough of Hammersmith and Fulham; Avril Lansdell, Curator of the Weybridge Museum; and, for help on various points, the late Raymond Mander and Joe Mitchenson, Richard Jeffree, Norman A. Josephs, and Lester S. Levy.

In its original form this study appeared in 1981 in a limited-circulation, typescript form. For this revised version I have been able to make a few small corrections and have also taken the opportunity to overhaul the material thoroughly. The major difference in content lies in the additional Chapter 4, on Kern's friends and private life in 1906—material that I have discovered since the original publication. For agreeing to publish this revised version I am grateful to H. Wiley Hitchcock and the Institute for Studies in American Music. Thanks to them, I am able to make the results of my research available in more elegant and permanent form as my own centenary tribute to one of the great geniuses of popular music.

Andrew Lamb
Croydon,
England
January 1985

1

INTRODUCTION

When Edward VII succeeded his mother, Queen Victoria, on the British throne in 1901, Jerome Kern was a sixteen-year-old living in Newark, New Jersey. Already he was beginning to demonstrate the talents that were to earn him recognition as one of America's very greatest popular-song composers. During that year he provided the music for a Newark High School production, *The Melodious Menu*.[2] Later the same year he was recruited by the Newark Yacht Club to provide the music for a dramatization of *Uncle Tom's Cabin*.[3]

Although his first published composition, the instrumental reverie *At the Casino*, appeared in 1902, Kern first began to achieve some sort of regular publication from late 1903, when he bought himself a junior partnership in the firm of T. B. Harms. Around the same time he began to get his songs accepted for interpolation into Broadway shows: *An English Daisy* at the Casino Theatre in early 1904, *Mr. Wix of Wickham* at the Bijou Theatre a few months later, and *The Silver Slipper* on a post-Broadway tour. Inevitably there were frustrations for a youngster struggling to establish himself. Thus "How'd You Like to Spoon With Me?" had to suffer rejection by Charles Frohman's New York manager Alf Hayman (see p. 44) before being accepted by the rival Shubert organization for interpolation into the American production of *The Earl and the Girl* in 1905, where it became Kern's first hit.

What all these Broadway shows had in common was a British origin. At that time the major musical shows produced in America were still imported from Europe, particularly from Britain. The attention that Charles Frohman, especially, gave to acquiring British shows for the American theater was no personal idiosyncracy, but a recognition of the dominant position that British popular musical shows occupied in the international musical theater. It is against this background that Kern's involvement in the London theater should be viewed.

The brand of musical comedy and musical play pioneered and perfected by the British impresario George Edwardes in the 1890s had enjoyed a vogue not only in

English-speaking countries but throughout the operetta theaters of the world. Sidney Jones's *The Geisha* in particular had achieved an international success matched by no other work of the British popular musical theater before it, not even *The Mikado*. In the ten years before *The Merry Widow* burst on the scene in 1906-7, the most traveled works of the international popular musical theater were those of Sidney Jones, Ivan Caryll, Lionel Monckton, Leslie Stuart, Howard Talbot, and Paul Rubens.

The most celebrated of London's musical shows in the early years of the century were those at George Edwardes's two flagship theaters, the Gaiety and Daly's. The former stood, increasingly remote from the main body of London's theaters, at the east end of the Strand. By the time that Jerome Kern visited London, the nineteenth-century Gaiety Theatre—little more than thirty years old—had been demolished to make way for a massive new street development and had been replaced by a new theater on the island site formed by the Strand and the newly created crescent-shaped thoroughfare, the Aldwych. The Gaiety offered a style of entertainment rich in fashionable dress, opulent staging, and, above all, shapely female beauty. Its musical format was descended from the older Gaiety burlesques, with operatic opening choruses and finales framing the cleverly contrived and tuneful song-and-dance numbers upon which—far more than any plot—the success of the show depended. By contrast, Daly's, at the northeast corner of Leicester Square, in the very heart of London's theaterland, offered a more sophisticated style of show— perhaps more elegant still, and with a greater consistency of plot and integration of musical score having rather more in common with the old comic opera style.

Elsewhere in London's theaterland were various other theaters that specialized in musical shows lying somewhere between those of the Gaiety and Daly's. Only a short distance from Daly's, to the west of Leicester Square and on the south side of Coventry Street, stood perhaps the most important of them, the Prince of Wales' Theatre, where Frank Curzon as manager and lessee staged a series of George Edwardes productions from 1903 to 1906 before embarking upon a series of his own. Curzon was also manager of the Criterion Theatre, only a short distance further along on the south side of Piccadilly Circus.

Slightly to the north, moving along Shaftesbury Avenue from Piccadilly Circus, one would come to the Lyric Theatre, which had a strong tradition of musical productions but was now alternating them with straight drama. A short distance further along was the Apollo Theatre, opened only in 1901. At both of these theaters George Edwardes mounted additional musical shows. Further along still, on the south side of Shaftesbury Avenue, was the old Shaftesbury Theatre (not the theater known by that name today), which at the turn of the century made a particular specialty, before returning to straight drama, of imported American musicals— Gustave Kerker's tremendously successful *The Belle of New York* in 1898 being followed in 1900 by the same composer's *An American Beauty* and Ludwig Englander's *The Casino Girl*, in 1903 by the black musical *In Dahomey*, and in 1904 by Gustav Luders's *The Prince of Pilsen*.

Further east, along the Strand towards the Gaiety, was the Vaudeville Theatre, which during the first years of the century was the base for the expanding London operations of the American manager Charles Frohman; these he conducted in conjunction with the theater's owners, the Gattis, and the actor-manager-author Seymour Hicks. Frohman's other London theater at the time was the Duke of York's in St. Martin's Lane, which staged mostly straight plays, being associated especially with J. M. Barrie's works, including *Peter Pan* in 1904.

Increasingly coming to the forefront of musical theatrical entertainment, however, were the big variety theaters, which enjoyed something of a heyday in the Edwardian era. The old Alhambra Theatre, on the east side of Leicester Square, had specialized in including spectacular ballet in its programs. In this it had been challenged successfully by George Edwardes's Empire Theatre of Varieties on the north side of the Square, almost alongside Daly's. Just to the northeast, where Shaftesbury Avenue meets Charing Cross Road at Cambridge Circus, was the Palace Theatre, built originally for Richard D'Oyly Carte as the English Opera House but by the 1900s presenting variety programs under the direction of the veteran Charles Morton, who was succeeded in 1904 by his assistant Alfred Butt. The increasing popularity of variety was demonstrated by the opening of the Coliseum in St. Martin's Lane at Christmas 1904.

Biographers have traditionally dated Kern's initial involvement with the London theater as 1903-4, representing this as the start of his association with Charles Frohman and his contribution of songs to various London shows. David Ewen, especially, has attributed specific songs to this period. In his first biography of Kern he states that "How'd You Like to Spoon With Me?" was written and first performed in London in 1903-4.[4] In later books he credits Kern with "My Little Canoe," sung by Billie Burke in *The School Girl*.[5] There and in still later writings he also associates this supposed 1903-4 visit with the song "Mr. Chamberlain," written with P. G. Wodehouse for a show Ewen amusingly cites as *The Beauty and the Bath*.[6]

In reality the published score of *The School Girl* readily demonstrates that "My Little Canoe," like the rest of the show's music, was by Leslie Stuart. Kern did write a song with a similar title—"Won't You Buy a Little Canoe?"—for a London show, but in 1906. Likewise, as Bordman rightly demonstrates, the show *The Beauty of Bath*, featuring "Mr. Chamberlain," was first produced only in 1906.[7] Moreover, as Bordman also demonstrates, it was only in 1905 that Kern obtained his agreement with Frohman to provide songs for the latter's shows.[8] As for "How'd You Like to Spoon With Me?," the following pages will demonstrate how vividly the British press reported its introduction into the London theater—again, in 1906. Thus, in every respect, the details Ewen produces in support of a 1903-4 visit by Kern to London may be shown to relate in fact to 1905-6.

Faced with this contradictory evidence, either of two conclusions might be drawn: either Kern did visit London in 1903-4 and the details quoted relate to a subsequent visit, or else the 1903-4 date is an error. In seeking to resolve the matter Bordman evidently made exhaustive efforts to substantiate a 1903-4 visit, even consulting passenger lists of Atlantic crossings on which Kern might have traveled with Frohman, in support of an anecdote that the two sailed back home together after their first meeting in London.[9] Yet his search for such evidence was apparently in vain, and he admits that "no incontestable evidence exists" for the traditional claim of a 1903-4 London visit.[10] Nor has the present writer found any evidence of such a London visit, whether in British sources or in the details of Kern's songwriting output (listed in Appendix 2 of this study), which will be shown to be generally an invaluable guide to Kern's London activities.

That Bordman nonetheless persists in accepting 1903-4 as the date of Kern's first visit to London he attributes to two reasons.[11] The first is the persistent rumors that Kern did his earliest work for London. The second is Kern's statement that his earliest musical comedy training was successively with Alfred Butt, Seymour Hicks, George Edwardes, and Charles Frohman—thereby implying, suggests Bordman, that his work was used by Butt before his involvement with the other managers.

In reality the first of these two reasons scarcely points one way more than the other. Whether in 1903 or 1905, Kern had already done some work in New York, and so the suggestion that he worked in London before New York cannot be taken as the literal truth. By 1905 he would hardly have considered himself much better established in New York than in 1903. As for the second reason, further examination reveals that, far from supporting Bordman's hypothesis, this too points in favor of 1905-6 rather than 1903-4. For one thing, it was only in 1904 that Alfred Butt became manager at the Palace Theatre, so that his would scarcely have been the name cited as advancing Kern's career in 1903-4. More positively, as the details to be presented in this study illustrate, Kern's association with Butt, just as with the other managers, can be dated as occurring in 1905-6 rather than 1903-4.

Can one, therefore, any longer doubt that the traditional dating of Jerome Kern's first involvement with the London theater is wrong? It is impossible to prove positively that Kern did *not* visit London in 1903-4. He may indeed have made a passing visit on his way to or from his alleged musical training in Germany. But it seems abundantly clear that 1905-6, if not the date of Kern's very first visit to London, was the start of his involvement with the West End theater.

2

PRODUCERS, THEATERS, AND SHOWS

That Kern was in London by the summer of 1905 is not open to doubt. It was then that he secured the agreement to provide songs for Charles Frohman's shows, as is confirmed by an announcement in the New York *Dramatic Mirror* of 15 July 1905 that is quoted by Bordman: "Jerome D. Kern, who, though not yet twenty-one, has composed several light operas and is a partner in a New York publishing house, has just been retained by Charles Frohman and Seymour Hicks for three years. Mr. Kern is to write for them twelve songs a year."[12]

To that point Kern's contributions to New York musical shows had amounted to no more than a few scattered songs, together with a substantial contribution to the undistinguished *Mr. Wix of Wickham*. Hence the agreement to provide songs for shows by a producer so active on both sides of the Atlantic as Charles Frohman was indeed a very significant step forward in the career of a young man still only twenty. Yet it poses significant questions in relation to Kern's activities. How was it that Kern managed to get alongside Frohman in London rather than New York? And what was Kern doing in London anyway?

The fact that Frohman and other producers were so dependent on British imports may have suggested to Kern the value of getting to know the British theater at first hand if he was to get his songs accepted by Frohman. The London theater of the early years of the century would have seemed a place of pilgrimage for any budding young theater composer, and Kern may also have recognized it as a place of opportunity. An essential feature of the George Edwardes musical was its allowance for the interpolation of extraneous songs by other than the nominal composers of a show. Increasingly America was seen as a source of suitable songs for such purposes. Having already achieved some small success with interpolations in New York, Kern might also have recognized the chance of something similar in London. Moreover, in view of the limited success that he had in getting Frohman's attention in New York, it may well have seemed that a better opportunity to do so existed in

London, where Frohman was by no means so well established: he was just then building up his London activities, with the construction of his own new theater, the Aldwych.

That Frohman was indeed actively seeking at that time to encourage new talent in London is made clear by a notice that appeared in the British theater and variety newspaper *The Era* on 17 June 1905: "Mr. Charles Frohman will run a school for musical comedy aspirants in connection with the new Aldwych Theatre, where novices will be prepared for parts in musical plays under the direction of that experienced actor Mr. Edward Royce. No fees will be required of the students, who will, moreover, be employed as supernumeraries at an adequate remuneration."[13] No doubt aspiring songwriters as well as actors were on Frohman's London shopping list.

As it happened, the first fruits of Kern's association with Frohman were heard not in London but in New York—in *The Catch of the Season* in August 1905 and in the Christmas production *The Babes and the Baron* in December 1905. Not until March 1906, apparently, did London first hear a contribution by Kern to a Frohman show, when *The Beauty of Bath*—which, like the aforementioned two works, had Herbert E. Haines as principal composer—opened at the new Aldwych Theatre. By that time, certainly, Kern's music had been used by Alfred Butt at the Palace Theatre, albeit in the form of a song that had already achieved success in America. Displaying an inability to get the song's title quite right that was typical of press reports of the time, *The Era* announced in its issue of Saturday, 10 February 1906:

> Miss Millie Legarde will make her appearance at the Palace on Monday in a new song, entitled "Won't you come and spoon by me?" It is of the "Sammy" order, and in its rendering the popular actress will have the assistance of a fascinating chorus of girls. Mr. Alfred Butt has secured the London rights of the song, which should be a great success.[14]

The following week the same paper gave an unusually detailed account of the song's presentation, but again failed to get the title quite right:

> Several novelties were introduced on Monday by Mr. Alfred Butt into the Palace programme at the Palace, where Miss Millie Legarde, an actress of considerable distinction and cleverness, is singing a new song that belongs to the same genre as "Sammy." It is of American brand, and is entitled "How'd you like to come and spoon with me?" The question is addressed to boxes, stalls, and gallery. On

the night to which we are now alluding, an occupant of a prompt side box evidently appreciated Miss Legarde's invitation, and gallantly assured her by eloquent pantomime of the conquest she had made. A stallite, on the contrary, took immediate flight – to the stage-door, perhaps; and one of the "gods" exclaimed with immense gusto, "Rather!" The actress looks very winsome and charming, and is beautifully gowned. She is also well supported by the eight Palace Girls, who form quite a galaxy of beauty.[15]

The song was without doubt a pronounced success, so much so that *The Era* had to return to it a fortnight later with a warning that at last enabled it to get the title right and also ensure that the composer did not go unnoticed:

We are asked by Mr. Alfred Butt to state that before Miss Millie Legarde sang "How'd you like to spoon with me?" at the Palace, the management purchased all performing rights within a six-mile radius of the theatre from Mr. Jerome D. Kern, the composer, and that permission to sing the number elsewhere within that area should be obtained from the Palace management. Mr. Butt is naturally anxious to avoid unpleasant proceedings against artists or brother managers.[16]

The success of the song was further confirmed by photographs of Millie Legarde that appeared in the weekly illustrated newspapers.[17] The text accompanying one in *The Tatler* gave a slightly different slant to the odd behavior of the fleeing stallite on the first night:

Thanks to Miss Millie Legarde's personality and striking style the song, "How'd You Like to Come and Spoon with Me?" which has created such a furore in America, promises to be one of the chief attractions at the Palace Theatre for some time to come. On the first night considerable amusement was occasioned by a young man in the audience, to whom she was more or less unconsciously addressing her question, being overcome with shyness, seizing his hat and making for the door.

As it happened, by the time this appeared Millie Legarde had ended her five-week engagement at the Palace on 17 March 1906. Only two nights later the first songs actually written for London by Kern were heard in *The Beauty of Bath*, the show mounted for Frohman at the Aldwych by his London manager Seymour Hicks and starring Hicks and his wife, Ellaline Terriss. Kern contributed two songs, for both of which P. G. Wodehouse had written (or, at any rate, revised) the lyrics. The first was the satirical political song "Mr. Chamberlain," sung by Hicks about the popular veteran reforming politician Joseph Chamberlain. The second was "The Frolic of a Breeze," a production number specially mounted by the theater's stage manager, Edward Royce, and performed by Bert Sinden bearing an umbrella and accompanied by a chorus of ladies bearing parasols.

In much later years Wodehouse referred to "Mr. Chamberlain" as having "a terrific tune,"[18] but one cannot help thinking that distance had lent a great deal of enchantment. It was very much the words of the song that mattered. In fact *The Times* (of London) dismissed the whole score with the opinion that "the tunes have no originality and not much melody to recommend them."[19] Interestingly, the only two numbers singled out for individual comment (albeit unfavorable) were the two Kern/Wodehouse ones, indicating, presumably, their role as special production numbers: "We wonder whether London in general is not as tired as we are of umbrella or parasol dances and songs about Mr. Chamberlain (last night's was much in the manner of the famous 'Mr. Dooley' song)." The theatrical paper *The Stage* was even blunter, maintaining that "the vocal portion . . . would certainly bear curtailing, and among the items to be thrown to the wolves might be Mr. Hicks's irrelevant 'Chamberlain' ditty and a foolish 'Flying Machine' concerted piece, both of which are in the vein of banal musical comedy."[20] *The Era* preferred to say nothing of Kern's contributions.[21]

If Kern's initiation into the more refined "musical play" was of limited critical success, he may have found himself more at home in the knockabout humor of musical comedy as mounted at the Gaiety Theatre. Bordman refers to "Rosalie" being sung there in *The Spring Chicken*, without establishing just when the song was added to the show.[22] One can, however, readily do so. It was the custom of the London theater of the time for a musical show to be rejuvenated occasionally by bringing out a "new edition" featuring new dialogue, new costumes, new scenery, new routines, and new songs. Thus *The Spring Chicken*, which had first been produced at the Gaiety Theatre on 30 May 1905, ran in a "new edition" on Thursday, 22 March 1906—just three days after the premiere of *The Beauty of Bath*. The following day's *Times* reviewed the new musical numbers: "Miss Gertie Millar scores most by the changes, for she gets two new songs for herself and a share in a quartet; but neither of her songs is so pretty as one called 'Rosalie' which Mr. George Grossmith jun. sings to a setting by Mr. Jerome K. Kern."[23]

That "Rosalie" was not Kern's only contribution to the new edition of *The Spring Chicken* we learn from *The Stage*, which gave a detailed account of the songs added.[24] Among them was " 'Gwendoline of Grosvenor Square' (words by G. Grossmith, jun., music by Jerome D. Kern), given near the end of the performance by Mr. Grossmith." The account goes on:

> Mr. Grossmith . . . also delivers pointedly another Gallic piece, "Rosalie," by the same collaborators, who are concerned further in "Sunday afternoon," in which on Thursday Mr. Grossmith and Mr. Payne made a tremendous hit, largely for the clever business introduced, including the former's take-off of Mr. Henry J. Wood conducting at Queen's Hall, with Mr. Payne playing the drum and triangle.

The Era agreed:

> The effervescing comicality of Mr. Edmund Payne in the part of the giddy Girdle has a new outlet in a duet called "Sunday afternoon," the success of which is shared by Mr. Geo. Grossmith, its author, as Babori. The various accessories of the number are inexpressibly droll, and the appearance of Mr. Payne as a fond papa out with the baby-chair and of Mr. Grossmith carrying the jug for the Sunday beer is irresistible.[25]

As for "Rosalie," *The Era* found it "full of unctuous humor."

Still more was to follow for Kern, however. On 17 April 1906 George Edwardes's Empire Theatre introduced *Venus, 1906*, a revue written once again by George Grossmith, Jr. One of the leading performers was the comedy actor W. H. Berry, who played several parts, which required quick changes of costume. In one scene he was a judge, in another a prehistoric policeman patrolling a prehistoric Trafalgar Square and combatting prehistoric monsters that emerged from behind boulders; in yet another he was a modern labor leader addressing a crowd at Speakers' Corner in Hyde Park and singing a Kern song, "The Leader of the Labour Party."[26] According to Berry's memoirs, one of the weekly magazines published a caricature of him in the role, dressed in a frock coat and cricket cap and carrying an umbrella.[27] In the final scene, Berry tells us, he was dressed as an American Indian in full war paint and feathers, and it was presumably in this role that Berry performed a second Kern song listed in the program, "Won't You Buy a Little Canoe?"[28]

This was not yet all for Kern. On 5 May, under the title of *A Girl on the Stage*, George Edwardes produced a substantially revised version of the Ivan Caryll musical *The Little Cherub*, which had been running at the Prince of Wales' Theatre since January. *The Stage* reported that "Mr. Caryll has written half a dozen fresh numbers, bright, tuneful, and pleasing; and Messrs. F. E. Tours and Jerome D. Kern have, between them, supplied half a dozen more. . . ."[29] Thus was Kern's name linked for the first time with that of Frank Tours, musical director at the Prince of Wales' Theatre, who was to remain a close associate of Kern for very many years. Unfortunately it is not clear just how many of their six numbers were contributed by Kern; but one, at any rate, is named in the *Stage* review. "Merry-go-round" is described as "a capital number, with a chorus to it, by Mr. Kern." It was sung by Gabrielle Ray, of whom *The Stage* went on to say that "her comely boy in 'Merry-go-round' is all lightsome jollity and nimble-footed energy."[30]

Thus, within the space of twelve weeks, Jerome Kern at the age of twenty-one had had songs performed at five London theaters—under the auspices of Alfred Butt at the Palace, Charles Frohman and Seymour Hicks at the Aldwych, and George Edwardes at the Gaiety, Empire, and Prince of Wales'. Can anyone possibly doubt that when, in later years, Kern recalled the early musical comedy training he had received from these producers it was this period in early 1906 to which he was referring?

3

LYRICISTS, SONGS, AND PUBLISHERS

Whatever Kern's personal ambitions may have had to do with his presence in London in 1905, he would scarcely have been able to indulge them if they had not coincided with the interests of his employer, T. B. Harms, on the income from whom he must have been dependent. Therein surely lies the real clue to his presence in London in 1905, and also the main reason why any earlier visit to London would have been unlikely. Prior to his partnership with Harms he would scarcely have had the means and, as we shall see, prior to 1905 scarcely the same business reasons for being in London.

For Harms, certainly, there would have been as much mileage as for Kern in finding a place in Frohman shows for songs that Kern would compose and Harms publish. And in 1905 their London connections would certainly have provided an opportunity to get alongside Frohman that probably did not exist in New York. Harms's London agent at the time was the leading firm of popular-song publishers, Francis, Day & Hunter. As it happened, Francis, Day & Hunter not only were the publishers of the current big London success of Frohman and Hicks, *The Catch of the Season* at the Vaudeville Theatre, but also had a substantial financial stake in the production.[31] It may thus have been through Francis, Day & Hunter that Kern, acting both as individual and on behalf of T. B. Harms, was able to get an introduction to Frohman in London in the spring of 1905.

But there were undoubtedly other reasons more directly related to Harms's current operations that brought about their need for a representative in London at that time. To appreciate these fully, it is worth looking, with particular reference to Kern's own compositions, at the role that Francis, Day & Hunter had been playing as Harms's London agent. As such, the firm was automatically sent a copy of each of Harms's publications for copyright deposit and possible British publication. Right from the start of Kern's association with T. B. Harms, proof copies of his published songs had been sent over to Francis, Day & Hunter and deposited for copyright registration in London on the same day as in Washington. The U.K. copyright copies of Kern's published songs from those earliest days may be seen today in the British Library, including 63 of them bound together in a single volume devoted exclusively to Kern.[32] In addition, the files of Francis, Day & Hunter (now part of EMI Music Publishing) contain additional proof copies of all eleven Kern numbers copyrighted in both Washington and London between December 1903 and May 1905. Of these eleven numbers, two were published by Francis, Day & Hunter in British editions. The first was "McGuire Esquire," a song about an aspiring tenor in a church choir. It was typical British music-hall material, and when the song was published by Francis, Day & Hunter the original two verses, with words by Kern, were supplemented by a further two by the firm's literary editor, Fred W. Leigh. This British edition, copyrighted in January 1905,[33] was the first song by Kern to be published in Britain, and it may even have been performed publicly in London at some variety theater or other.

The second of these early Harms publications of Kern songs to be published in a British edition was none other than "How'd You Like to Spoon With Me?" Bordman refers to the song's introduction into *The Earl and the Girl* in New York in November 1905;[34] however, the song's lyricist Edward Laska made clear in an article on the song's origins published in *Variety*[35] that the show and the song had opened in Chicago some time previously. Indeed, news of the song's success had crossed the Atlantic several months before the New York opening. In its issue of 22 April 1905 *The Era* reported that "one of the greatest song successes of *The Earl and the Girl*, as produced in America, is a charming number, by Edward Laska and Jerome D. Kern, entitled 'How'd you like to spoon with me?' sung by Miss Georgia Caine and Mr. Victor Morley."[36] The copyright deposit copies of the Harms edition, already showing the song as sung by two characters in *The Earl and the Girl*, were registered for copyright in both Washington and London as early as 21 March 1905.

The news item about "How'd You Like to Spoon With Me?" in *The Era* would doubtless have been a "plug" by Francis, Day & Hunter, who duly brought out their own edition, which they listed among their "summer specialities" in *The Era* on 13 May 1905.[37] A copy was deposited at the British Library for copyright registration on 6 June—which, it should be noted, was more than seven months before the song was launched at the Palace Theatre. It would seem that the song made no particular mark in London until the performances there the following year, whereupon Francis, Day & Hunter reprinted it and brought it out as no. 258 of their Sixpenny [£0.025] Popular Editions, a series of cheap reprints of their more successful popular songs which had been launched to combat the sale of pirated editions of popular music that flourished in London from about the turn of the century. An illustration of the popular impact the song then made is provided by a cartoon that appeared in *Cassell's Magazine* in February 1907.[38] Designed to highlight the absurdity of popular-song titles in incongruous situations, it depicted a well-dressed couple observing a disheveled popular-music seller crying his wares: " ' 'Owd Yer Like to Spoon Wid Me?' 'In the Shade o' the Ole Apple Tree'."

In the spring of 1905, however, there was one specific item of Harms business with Francis, Day & Hunter that demanded attention. In the issue of *The Era* with the item about the American success of "How'd You Like to Spoon With Me?" (22 April 1905)—indeed, in the column next to it—there appears an item about a visit to New York by David Day, head of Francis, Day & Hunter.[39] The purpose of the visit is reported to be "clearing up" with firms who had acted as American agents of Francis, Day & Hunter, in view of the setting up of a New York branch of the firm. While in New York, *The Era* further reported, Day was also promoting the scheme of reciprocation whereby the American rights of British successes were exchanged for the British rights of American songs.

T. B. Harms would of course have been one of the firms with which David Day "cleared up," as a result of which they would lose the reciprocation benefits they had hitherto enjoyed. In order to maintain a cross-Atlantic representation and reciprocation Harms thus required a link-up with another London firm. It would seem that the person sent over to London to arrange it was none other than Kern.

The parting of Harms from Francis, Day & Hunter was obviously a perfectly amicable one, and Kern's first business visit in London would doubtless have been to the latter's premises in Charing Cross Road. There he would have met not only members of the ruling Francis and Day families but also such employees as the literary editor Fred W. Leigh, who had written those extra verses for "McGuire Esquire." And perhaps it was only natural that they should decide upon a collaboration. Together they wrote "Won't You Kiss Me Once Before You Go?" which was published by Francis, Day & Hunter and copyrighted on 24 July 1905. The song is another typical British music-hall song of the time, and its title seems deliberately to have been designed to capture the lilt and flavor of "How'd You Like to Spoon With Me?"

In recording that "Won't You Kiss Me Once Before You Go?" was used in the New York production of *The Catch of the Season*, Bordman gives the song's lyricist as Charles H. Taylor rather than Leigh, presumably on the basis of the American edition.[40] It was not unknown at the time for Francis, Day & Hunter songs to be given two sets of lyrics—in this case a standard one by Leigh for general use and another by Taylor for topical theatrical use. That Leigh's claim to "Won't You Kiss Me Once Before You Go?" should take priority over Taylor's is indicated not only by his version being submitted for the original British copyright but also by the U.S. copyright being renewed in 1932 in the name of Jerome Kern and Kate Leigh; presumably she was the widow or other relation of Leigh, who had died in 1924.

One less predictable result of Kern's association with Francis, Day & Hunter is revealed in *The Era* of 24 June 1905 in connection with an announcement that both of the firm's London establishments would be closed all that day for the firm's fourth annual staff outing.[41] The party was to leave London Bridge Station at 9:25 a.m., their destination being the Burford Bridge Hotel at Box Hill in Surrey (still today a popular place for a summer outing). A full program of sports had been arranged by a committee that included "the genial Fred W. Leigh, whose gift of humour is nearly, if not quite, surpassed by his vein of poetic tenderness." And among the honored guests were to be not only David Day and William Francis, founding fathers of the firm, but "Mr. Jerome D. Kern, representing T. B. Harms & Co. of New York." The report of the occasion in the following week's issue of *The Era* [42] makes no mention of Kern, and so it is impossible to know how he may have performed in the egg-and-spoon race and other events—or, indeed, whether he actually attended. However, a fine time was apparently had by all. At the end of the proceedings a toast was proposed "to absent members, referring especially to the firm in America, where Mr. Fred Day has started business, and cheers were given for him and Mr. William Francis jun. who shares in his responsibility."

Meanwhile, Kern would have been making arrangements for T. B. Harms's new London representation. The firm with which Harms now established a reciprocal agency was Hopwood & Crew, whose U.S. agent had until then been the White-Smith Music Publishing Co. of Boston, New York, and Chicago. And it seems entirely consistent with the paths that both Kern and Harms were following that the firm was one of the leading London publishers of musical comedy scores of the time, including the most recent Seymour Hicks production at the Lyric Theatre, *The Talk of the Town.*

Hopwood & Crew immediately marked the new relationship with Kern and Harms by preparing printing plates for no fewer than five of Kern's songs. Proof copies of all five were deposited at the British Library for copyright registration in Harms's name on 20 July 1905. Of the five, one ("Raining") went straight into the American version of *The Catch of the Season*, while a further two ("The Frolic of a Breeze" and "Oh! Mr. Chamberlain") were eventually revised in collaboration with P. G. Wodehouse for the London production of *The Beauty of Bath*. A fourth, "The Bagpipe Serenade," had to wait fifteen months before finding a place in *The Rich Mr. Hoggenheimer* in America, while the fifth, "Tulips (Two Lips)," seems never to have been used in a show at all.

For a London publisher to prepare printing plates and proof copies for copyright in an American publisher's name was a highly unusual occurrence, and it suggests something of the very special nature of the contact between Kern, T. B. Harms, and Hopwood & Crew. That printing plates of the five songs should have been prepared at all by Hopwood & Crew suggests they had some expectation of publishing them in due course and thus that the songs had probably already been accepted by Frohman for his shows. Moreover, the fact that in none of the five songs was an American collaborator involved suggests that they had been written or completed in London. Both "The Bagpipe Serenade" and "Tulips (Two Lips)" had lyrics by Kern himself, while "The Frolic of a Breeze" and "Raining" had lyrics—initially at least—by F. Clifford Harris, one of Hopwood & Crew's regular lyricists. As for "Oh! Mr. Chamberlain," the proof copy in the British Library credits the lyric to Charles H. Taylor but actually contains no words at all. Apparently the published American edition has words by F. Clifford Harris,[43] while that finally used in *The Beauty of Bath* has words credited jointly to Kern and P. G. Wodehouse. Doubtless it was intended that (like "Won't You Kiss Me Once Before You Go?") the song should have a standard set of words, to be replaced for the theater by a topical set by Charles H. Taylor. In the event, the job of providing the theatrical set fell to Wodehouse, apparently aided by Kern, who may indeed have provided the original dummy lyric.

What is particularly noteworthy about the five songs is their overtly British nature. "Oh! Mr. Chamberlain," of course, is a satire of a leading British politician of the time, while "The Bagpipe Serenade" contains quotations of the Scottish airs "The Campbells Are Coming" and "Comin' Thru the Rye." "The Frolic of a Breeze" and "Raining" would both seem to have offered material for the umbrella or parasol dances that the *Times* reviewer the following March implied were so much in vogue in the British theater (see p. 9). It seems clear that these five songs were designed very specifically as test pieces for Frohman with London audiences in mind.

Moreover, their consciously British connotations may have some relevance to the story, quoted by Bordman, whereby Frohman mistook Kern for an Englishman and invited him to accompany him back to America: "Only as they reached New York did Frohman realize his Englishman was a Yankee."[44] Bordman insists that this story "should be put to rest." Yet, in view of the very definite British nature of the songs Kern presented to Frohman as test pieces in London, is it not easy to believe that there is at least some element of truth in the story of Frohman mistaking Kern for an Englishman?

Whether indeed Frohman and Kern traveled together back to New York seems unclear. However, it should be pointed out that, whereas Bordman seeks to find the common Atlantic crossing that allegedly followed their first meeting as occurring in July 1904, it would have been a year later (if it indeed occurred). As for 1905, Bordman states that Kern was aboard neither the *Philadelphia*, which sailed on 7 July 1905, nor the *Kronprinz Wilhelm*, on which Frohman sailed on 25 July.[45] However, it is difficult to reject entirely the statement by the New York *Dramatic Mirror* to the effect that Kern returned to America during July 1905.[46] It would have been logical for him to have done so, with both the Harms agency and the agreement with Frohman tied up.

Kern would almost certainly have been back in New York for the publication, in September and October 1905, of a few further songs that probably had their origins in the London trip. These were now sent over for copyright registration in London—not to Francis, Day & Hunter but to Hopwood & Crew. For "Take Me on the Merry-Go-Round," "Molly O'Hallerhan," and, apparently, "An Autumn Bud" Kern was again his own lyricist. The first of these was presumably the song that was used the following year in the London show *A Girl on the Stage*. The second was for the American version of *The Catch of the Season* and, as Bordman records,[47] saw Kern "paraphrasing small sections of both . . . music and lyric" of the song "Molly O'Halloran" in the British version of that show which he would doubtless have seen in London.

As will later be shown, Kern was back in London around the very beginning of 1906. During this further visit he may have worked again with F. Clifford Harris, producing the song "Meet Me at Twilight," which was used later in the year in the American production of *The Little Cherub*. It was probably also early in 1906 (although possibly already in 1905) that Kern met and worked with George Grossmith on their collaborations for *The Spring Chicken* at the Gaiety and *Venus, 1906* at the Empire.

In Grossmith, Kern found someone who was to be of immediate and lasting importance in furthering his cause in London. Grossmith's importance as leading man at the Gaiety, as well as book author and lyricist, might have been sufficient in itself; but in addition he had a penchant for introducing American songs into British shows. How this came about Grossmith explains in his autobiography.[48] Despite his being leading man at the Gaiety, he found that most of the best numbers composed by the principal British musical-comedy songwriter of the time, Lionel Monckton, were appropriated by the leading lady, Gertie Millar, who happened to be Mrs. Lionel Monckton. Thus Grossmith became accustomed to looking to America for songs to introduce into his performances, among them Jean Schwartz's "Mr. Dooley" and "Bedelia." Hence, perhaps, the interest that he evidently now felt in the young American composer over in London.

Grossmith provides a recollection of working with Kern in those early days in London. *Pace* David Ewen,[49] this offers further support for the idea that Kern's involvement with London did not begin until 1905:

> Somewhere between the years 1905-1910 there was a penniless little Jewish song writer who hailed from America, but made his home in London. I knew him as Jerry Kern and liked him immensely. He came often to my house and played to us. He played divinely like nearly all of his kind, with a tremendous gift of "tune." He was the only one I could detect in a barren field likely to fill the shoes of Monckton, Paul Rubens, and Leslie Stuart. In my dressing-room at the Gaiety was a tiny yacht piano on which Paul Rubens had composed his first song that was sung in a London theatre – "Trixie from the Town of Upper Tooting."[50]

> "Give me a lyric," one night asked Jerry, "and let me try what I can do on the same instrument"; and together we wrote and composed "Rosalie," which I sang in, I think, *The Spring Chicken*.[51]

Certainly it was in March 1906 that Kern first met P. G. Wodehouse, when the latter was offered by Seymour Hicks the position that Wodehouse recorded in his diary on 6 March as being "Regular job at £2 a week, starting with the run of *The Beauty of Bath* (March 19th) to do topical verses etc."[52] As Wodehouse later recalled, he first met Kern inside the Aldwych Theatre, where the latter, in his shirtsleeves, was playing poker with several of the actors.[53] (Kern's interest in this card game was illustrated later in the same year by the "card duet" "Poker Love" he composed for *The Rich Mr. Hoggenheimer*.) Only in those final two weeks before *The Beauty of Bath* came before the public could Wodehouse have been involved in revising the lyrics of the two Kern songs "Mr. Chamberlain" and "The Frolic of a Breeze," which had already been printed in their original form as much as eight months earlier.

4

FRIENDS, NIGHTLIFE, AND BOOK COLLECTING

Of Kern's private life as a young man in London his biographers tell us nothing prior to his meeting his future wife. Yet thanks to a little-known book of reminiscences we learn quite a lot about this aspect of his time in London. The author of the book was one Bertie Hollender.[54] His prime object in life was apparently to enjoy himself, and his memoirs are of the slightest, most gossipy, and hastily written kind. By a stroke of good fortune, however, one of his closest friends in his pleasure-seeking days in London in the early years of this century was Jerome Kern.

Hollender tells us that he and Kern were half of a quartet of close companions.[55] Both of the others were Americans—Raymond Howard, "a most amusing fellow . . . , the son of the then well-known jeweller in Fifth Avenue," and Powers Gouraud, a member of one of New York's socialite families and "one of the funniest white men living." How Hollender came to fall in with these three Americans he does not state. It seems likely, however, that contact was made during a spell that Hollender had in New York around 1903. One priceless piece of information that Hollender does provide is that, at least in the early months of 1906, Kern and Raymond Howard shared a flat in Jermyn Street.[56] Jermyn Street lies immediately to the south of Piccadilly and runs parallel to it, between St. James's Street and the Haymarket. (Benjamin Franklin lodged there in 1725.) Unfortunately, no *Post Office London Street Directory* of the early years of this century discloses the precise address of Kern and Howard. That it was an ideal base for Kern's theatrical activities, however, is clear, for one of the street's residents was Frank Curzon, manager of the Criterion and Prince of Wales' theaters. A few paces northwards from Jermyn Street would have brought Kern to Piccadilly Circus itself, the center of London's nightlife, from where London's theaterland stretched out along Coventry Street to Leicester Square, or along Shaftesbury Avenue. A short distance further, up Charing Cross Road, would have brought him by day to Francis, Day & Hunter's premises. Kern must have walked these routes many times.

But it was not only for theaters and music publishers that Kern's Jermyn Street address would have proved so handy. Adjoining the Prince of Wales' Theatre, on that short stretch between Piccadilly Circus and Leicester Square, stood Princes Building, which housed the premises of the Walsingham Club, of which Hollender tells us Kern was a member.[57] According to Hollender, the club's "Kitchen," a room filled with barrels of beer and representing an old-fashioned tavern, was one of the fashionable places to have supper in those days. Many of the club's members appear to have had theatrical connections; among them was Lennox Pawle, who early in 1906 had a leading role in *The Little Cherub* at the Prince of Wales' Theatre next door. Hollender adds that a great feature of the club was the Sunday concerts, when ladies were allowed in and first-class entertainment was provided.

By day Kern would also have found yet another diversion along those well-trodden routes, as we learn not from Hollender, but from George Grossmith: "Even in his struggling days in London when a pound or two meant much to him, he managed to save and out of those savings to buy and treasure – a book. Maybe, at first, some bargain of merit in excellent condition and binding for a few shillings at a second hand shop. Then some folio – bidden for – little competition – no reserve – at Putticks."[58] Charing Cross Road was then, as now, the home of many of London's second-hand bookshops, while Puttick and Simpson, auctioneers, were to be found at 47 Leicester Square, just around the corner from the Prince of Wales' Theatre and the Walsingham Club.

Grossmith's reference to Kern collecting books during those early days in London apparently contradicts Bordman's suggestion that the hobby began years later in New York.[59] According to Bordman, Kern was introduced to the hobby by Harry B. Smith, with whom Kern did not collaborate until 1913. However, there is no reason why Kern should not have met Smith earlier. Indeed it is scarcely to be imagined that he could have failed to do so, for example, when both were involved with *The Rich Mr. Hoggenheimer* in 1906. In any case Bordman acknowledges that Kern had already begun collecting in a small way before Smith fostered the interest. It seems entirely reasonable that Kern's strolls around London's Leicester Square and Charing Cross Road had nurtured the interest and that these English origins help to explain the strong emphasis on English literature in Kern's celebrated collection.

The flat in Jermyn Street was also a convenient starting-point from which to set out on some sudden youthful escapade. Hollender tells us of one occasion when, around 12:30 at night, two of the friends dashed into his room and announced that they were all going for an all-night drive, having wired to a place called The King of Prussia at High Wycombe to prepare breakfast for them.[60] They were to go in two cars, with eight in the party—the four men and four girls from the Gaiety whom Hollender describes as "good friends of ours and real sports." Apparently Hollender, like Raymond Howard, was given no time to dress beyond throwing his overcoat over his pajamas. He goes on to relate that, having reached The King of Prussia, the group was forced to wait for breakfast while the proprietor's wife showed off her young daughter's talents in reciting "Twinkle, twinkle, little star." When eventually breakfast was served and eaten, the party set off back to London, only to find themselves in the middle of campaigning for a local election. Full of high spirits, they parked their cars opposite each other and the two sets of occupants set about haranguing each other on behalf of the election candidates. Raymond Howard, meanwhile, still dressed in his pajamas, was dancing and playing wildly on his violin, which he apparently took with him wherever he went. Only when the police arrived to break up the crowd of villagers and a party of astonished schoolboys who had gathered to watch did the party resume its journey back to London. There, having delivered the ladies back to their homes, the four men retired for some further drinking at the Walsingham Club.

In the course of his account Hollender reveals that the names of the two election candidates were Herbert and Cripps. One can thereby date the episode as occurring in the run-up to the general election of January 1906. In that election the seat for the South (or Wycombe) Division of Buckinghamshire was gained by the Liberal Party candidate, Thomas Arnold Herbert, from the Unionist candidate, Seddon Cripps. *The Times* described the local campaign as "the most exciting experienced for many years"[61] and incidentally reported on a novel method used by the Liberal candidate to cover the widely scattered constituency: "He spoke three speeches into a phonograph, and the words are being taken round the villages of South Bucks and are being reproduced nightly. Between the phonograph speeches band selections, songs, &c are given from the same instrument."[62]

Thus did Kern have at least some marginal exposure to the British general election of 1906, from which derived the significance not so much of "Mr. Chamberlain" in *The Beauty of Bath* as "The Leader of the Labour Party" in *Venus, 1906*. It was in the 1906 election that the Labour Party achieved its first representation in the British Parliament. (Incidentally, The King of Prussia still stands today, though under a different name. Political developments prior to World War I caused it to change its name first to The Old King of Prussia and later to The King George V; as such it may still be found on the London Road, leading into High Wycombe.)

In considering the date of this episode, it is also of interest to reflect that, being in London in January 1906, Kern must apparently have celebrated his twenty-first birthday there.

The flat in Jermyn Street was also, it seems, the setting for many an evening's musical entertainment. Kern was, Hollender states, "a magnificent musician," while Raymond Howard "was quite a performer on the violin" and Powers Gouraud "became later quite a well-known amateur songwriter."[63] There are links here with Kern's published output. For *The Little Cherub* in 1906 Kern produced a song called "A Plain Rustic Ride," of which Bordman was unable to trace a copy but which he describes as having "a lyric by someone identified only as Gounard."[64] There is, however, a copyright deposit copy of this song in the British Library, and it shows that the lyricist was none other than Jerome D. Kern; the music is a collaboration between Kern and the "coon song" composer Jackson Gouraud. The latter features in Hollender's memoirs as another member of Powers Gouraud's family, and the husband of the American socialite Aimée Crocker.[65] As for Raymond Howard and his violin playing, could he perhaps have been related to the Arthur Platt Howard who wrote the words of "An Evening Hymn," with violin or flute obbligato, that most atypical of Kern's compositions, which was deposited for copyright in December 1905?

At all events, it was certainly these musical gatherings in the Jermyn Street flat that led to songs by Kern finding their way into various London theaters. Hollender tells us that it was he who introduced Kern to George Grossmith, Jr.; he recalls:

> Jerry had written quite a few good numbers and didn't know where to place them. One of them was called "Charlotte the Harlot." He was dreadfully hard up in those days, like most of us, and one day I suggested taking him into George Grossmith's dressing-room at the Gaiety. We arrived there and I asked him to play George a tune or so. George had a piano in his dressing-room. To make a long story short, "Charlotte the Harlot" went into the Gaiety show, the music being the same but, curiously enough, they changed our lyrics.[66]

What song "Charlotte the Harlot" may have become is scarcely to be determined now. In respect of another debt Kern apparently owed to Hollender, however, we can be more specific, for it is possible to deduce from Hollender's book that he was probably also responsible for getting Kern his introduction to Alfred Butt and the Palace Theatre. It seems that Hollender's father, Max Holländer, was chairman of the Palace Theatre Company and as such had been responsible for bringing Butt to the Palace from his previous position as accountant at Harrod's store.[67] What is more, Hollender tells us that, on the first night of Millie Legarde's performance of "How'd You Like to Spoon With Me?" at the Palace, the four friends were all in a stage box,[68] and he recalls that "the overtures from the singer were rather embarrassing." The full significance of this information may begin to dawn if we recall the account of the song's first-night reception that was published in *The Era* (see pp. 7–8). Was it, perhaps, one of Kern's and Hollender's party who, in the words of *The Era*, "appreciated Miss Legarde's invitation and gallantly assured her of the conquest she had made"? Remarkably, the matter can be resolved beyond serious doubt. *The Era*'s vivid account is fascinatingly complemented by a photograph that appeared in the pictorial weekly *The Sketch*, showing Miss Legarde singing "How'd You Like to Spoon With Me?" and beckoning across the orchestra to four young men in evening dress in a stage box.[69] Although the photograph has been given renewed currency in recent times by being reproduced by Raymond Mander and Joe Mitchenson in the original edition of their *British Music Hall*,[70] neither they nor anyone else seems to have given much attention to the identity of the four young men. Yet the young man second from the left is quite clearly identifiable as Jerome Kern. Presumably the other three were the other members of Kern's little group of friends. Indeed, comparison with a self-portrait of Bertie Hollender in his book[71] seems to confirm that he is the man on the extreme left, leaning out of the box. Evidently it was he who had responded so positively to Millie Legarde's overtures.

Here, then, is remarkable documentation of the twenty-one-year-old Jerome Kern, still virtually unknown, and yet pictured in the press at the Palace Theatre, London, on 12 February 1906, listening with his friends to what was possibly the very first public performance of his music in the British capital.

5

INTERLUDE

It is, of course, impossible to know the full extent of Kern's theatergoing on these early visits to London. It seems reasonable to assume, however, that it would have been substantial. During his 1905 visit, for instance, he could have seen *The Catch of the Season*, already past its 300th performance at the Vaudeville Theatre. At George Edwardes's Gaiety Theatre he might even have been around on 30 May 1905 for the first night of *The Spring Chicken*, that show with book by Grossmith and music by Caryll and Monckton for which he would soon be contributing some songs. At the Prince of Wales' Theatre he could have appreciated the all-round talents of book author/lyricist/composer Paul A. Rubens in *Lady Madcap*, which in America became *My Lady's Maid*. Doubtless, too, he investigated the entertainments at the variety theaters—the Alhambra, Empire, and newly opened Coliseum, as well as the Palace. One can imagine him being less taken, perhaps, by the more ambitiously composed works at Daly's and the Apollo— *The Little Michus* and *Véronique*—both of them adaptations of French works with scores by André Messager, who was then director of Covent Garden Opera.

On his return to London in early 1906 Kern could have seen Ivan Caryll's *The Little Cherub* around the time of its first night at the Prince of Wales' Theatre on 13 January 1906. He could also have seen the tail end of Howard Talbot's *The White Chrysanthemum* at the Criterion Theatre. Before he returned home he could have caught the first nights of a string of new shows: Leslie Stuart's *The Belle of Mayfair* at the Vaudeville on 11 April, *The Dairymaids* with music by Rubens and Frank E. Tours at the Apollo on 14 April, and *The Girl Behind the Counter* with music by Howard Talbot at Wyndham's on 21 April.

Of recurrent interest in considering the musical shows he might have seen in London is the way in which so many of them cropped up again in his future output— most immediately in the form of shows for the American productions of which he was to provide interpolated numbers. One work that may have made a particular impression on him was the one that separated *Véronique* and *The Dairymaids* at the Apollo. This was *Mr. Popple (of Ippleton)*, another work with book, music, and lyrics by Paul A. Rubens. What was significant about the show was that, as Rubens himself stressed, it was not a comic opera or musical comedy with opulent staging and big chorus numbers but, as he called it, a "comedy with music."[72] His avowed aim had been to write a comedy with a consistent story that achieved its effect "without wanting a string of musical numbers, a large chorus, and scenery and dresses which are so costly that only a very long run can compensate the management for its lavish expenditure." Perhaps Rubens was ahead of his time—certainly *Mr. Popple's* replacement, *The Dairymaids*, was a reversion to the conventionally opulent style of musical play—but his ideas of a more intimate musical production must have struck a chord in the mind of the young Jerome Kern. Nine years later *Mr. Popple (of Ippleton)* was adapted by Guy Bolton, provided with new songs by Kern, and produced in New York as *Nobody Home*, the first of those Princess Theatre shows that have come to be regarded as pioneering efforts in the development of a modern form of musical comedy.

For the moment, however, it was the more traditional form of musical comedy and musical play that was imported from Britain by Frohman and the rival Shubert organization. And, thanks to the agreement with Frohman that Kern had achieved in London, he was now called upon with some regularity to provide additional numbers for these American adaptations. Whatever may have been the intention when Kern had those original songs accepted by Frohman and Hicks back in 1905, Frohman seems to have decided at an early stage that he could make better use of Kern's talents by using his songs for his American rather than his British productions. Though Kern was to collaborate again with British lyricists in London over the next few years, the resultant songs were used almost exclusively for American productions. One purpose of Kern's subsequent visits to London as a young man, beyond his work for T. B. Harms, may have been to see shows that would subsequently be produced in America and thereby to be better equipped to write songs for interpolation at particular points in their action.

Evidence of any further visit by Kern to London during 1906 and 1907 appears to be nonexistent. The list of his published songs suggests an entirely American involvement. Thus, after his return to New York from London in 1906, he would have been able to concentrate on building upon the experience he had gained with Alfred Butt, Seymour Hicks, and George Edwardes. Besides songs for Englander's *The Rich Mr. Hoggenheimer* and Kerker's *Fascinating Flora*, there were others for the American productions of *The Little Cherub, My Lady's Maid, The White*

Chrysanthemum, *The Orchid*, and *The Dairymaids*, almost all of them shows he probably had seen in London. In addition, during this period he appears to have made a vaudeville tour as accompanist to Edna Wallace Hopper, marked by the dedication of the song "Blue, Blue!" to "E. W-H."

Proof copies of all these songs continued to be sent to England by Harms for copyright registration in London by Hopwood & Crew or, after their merger with E. Ascherberg & Co. in 1906, by Ascherberg, Hopwood & Crew. From Kern's association with this firm not merely do the Harms proof copies in the British Library survive but also the records of the firm itself, now absorbed into Chappell International. The stock books show that of the five songs of which Hopwood & Crew had prepared printing plates and proof copies for copyright deposit in July 1905 only "Mr. Chamberlain" was ever actually published as a separate number, though "The Frolic of a Breeze" appeared with it in the score of *The Beauty of Bath*. Of the separate issue of "Mr. Chamberlain," only 300 copies were printed, in June 1906, then 250 more in November. Of course, such was the pricing structure of the time that few would opt for a single number at two shillings (£0.10) rather than the complete vocal score at five shillings (£0.25)—which, with beautifully illustrated cover, sold many thousands of copies.

Of a further 36 Kern songs of which proof copies from Harms were deposited for copyright registration in England by Hopwood & Crew (or Ascherberg, Hopwood & Crew) between 1905 and 1908, only four were published in Britain. "Meet Me at Twilight," Kern's last collaboration with Clifford Harris, managed a print run of 250 copies in April 1907 (apparently in conjunction with the song's being used in a touring British musical, *The Maid and the Motorman*), and a further 500 in a cheap edition at one shilling (£0.05) the following March. In August 1907 "Don't You Want a Paper, Dearie?" and "Ballooning," two songs with lyrics by Paul West, each achieved single printings of 500 copies, possibly also in connection with their use in a British show. Not even the ploy of exploiting the opening of London's newest underground railway by issuing "The Subway Express" (lyric by James O'Dea) under the title "Bakerloo (The Subway Express)" in October 1907 produced a print of more than 500 copies. Though "Rosalie" had meanwhile been published in London by Chappell and "How'd You Like to Spoon With Me?" continued to enjoy popularity, recognition of Kern seems once more to have been making more progress in America than in Britain.

6

RETURN VISIT

Bordman suggests that, with the death of his mother in December 1907 and his father's final illness, Kern's career "came to an abrupt halt" and that he cancelled plans for another trip to London.[73] However, the evidence is that Kern did make a visit to London—and an extended one—in the first half of 1908. The primary evidence is the list of his compositions, which once again shows a sequence of collaborations with British lyricists that could only be consistent with a period of work in London. Thus, of fourteen songs copyrighted between August and October 1908, no fewer than eleven had British lyricists. The lyrics of nine were contributed by C. H. Bovill, who had by then joined Frohman's team of London writers.

It would have been logical for Kern to wish to get back to London in 1908 to catch up on the latest productions there. At the Prince of Wales' Theatre *Miss Hook of Holland*, another one-man book/lyrics/music creation of Paul Rubens, was followed on 21 April by yet another Rubens piece, *My Mimosa Maid*. Of the two principal George Edwardes theaters, the Gaiety was staging a further Grossmith/Caryll/Monckton work, *The Girls of Gottenberg*, to be followed on 25 April by Leslie Stuart's *Havana*. At Daly's the show that was to signal the eclipse of the British musical play—*The Merry Widow*—was firmly ensconced.

Kern's attention would no doubt have centered upon the productions of the Frohman/Hicks organization. At the Aldwych *The Gay Gordons*, with a Scottish setting, had music by Guy Jones (brother of Sidney) and some lyrics by C. H. Bovill and P. G. Wodehouse, with Kern's future collaborators Frank Tours as conductor and Edward Royce as stage manager. Since Kern's previous visit, Frohman had added yet another new theater, the Hicks (now the Globe) in Shaftesbury Avenue. Opened in 1906 with a transfer of *The Beauty of Bath* from the Aldwych, it had then presented the less successful final collaboration of Charles H. Taylor and Herbert E. Haines, *My Darling*, followed by the non-musical *Brewster's Millions*. Kern may well have caught the tail end of the last-named and remembered it when he came to set a musical adaptation of the piece as *Zip Goes a Million* in 1919.

Of prime interest, however, would doubtless have been the new show that opened at the Hicks Theatre on 7 March. The Edwardes and Frohman organizations had pooled their resources for Oscar Straus's *A Waltz Dream*, and some George Edwardes favorites, notably George Grossmith and Gertie Millar, had been imported from the Gaiety to add strength to the production. What would have made it of particular interest to Kern was that he apparently once again had at least one song in a London show. When the monthly *The Play Pictorial* of 1 May 1908 featured *A Waltz Dream* it devoted a whole page to a portrait of Grossmith in the role of Count Lothario and an extended quotation of the Bovill/Kern song "The Gay Lothario."[74]

What is unusual about this song quotation is that it is not set in type, as was customary in *The Play Pictorial*, but reproduced from manuscript, in piano-vocal score with some indications of orchestration. The fact that it is in manuscript suggests that the song had been written with Bovill during the 1908 visit to London and was still too new for Kern to have sent back to New York for typesetting. The printed Harms edition was eventually deposited for copyright in October 1908, along with two other songs for *A Waltz Dream*—"I'd Much Rather Stay at Home" and "Vienna." These, too, were written with British lyricists—the former with Bovill and the latter with Adrian Ross, the principal lyricist of the British adaptation. These songs, too, may have been used in the London production, though press reports provide no positive confirmation. But it seems right to question Bordman's statement that "Vienna" and one other song had been included in the New York production of *A Waltz Dream* in January 1908.[75] It is difficult to ignore the evidence of the lyricists' identity and the copyright dates to the effect that the songs were probably written in Britain in 1908. Of course, they may well have been added to the American production at a later date.

Of the use of Kern songs in another London show in 1908 we can be more definite. On 5 May the Queen's Theatre in Shaftesbury Avenue staged a revival of *The Dairymaids*, and into the Rubens and Tours score Kern managed to insert two of the numbers originally used in the 1907 American production of the show. *The Stage* reported their performance by the light comedy pair of Florence Lloyd and Dan Rolyat:

> . . . Miss Lloyd and Mr. Rolyat have two good numbers in the "Hay ride," where they come in on a little cart drawn by a donkey, and in "I'd like to meet your father," also with business of the modern musical comedy sort. The music of this and of the "Hay ride," not the least taking in the piece, was written by Jerome Kern. . . . [76]

Besides the songs for *A Waltz Dream*, there were other songs by Kern from the 1908 London visit, with lyrics by Bovill and George Grossmith, that were to find their way into the American production of *The Girls of Gottenberg*. But the show for which the bulk of Kern's 1908 collaborations with Bovill and Grossmith were to be used was *Fluffy Ruffles*, in which Grossmith himself was to appear in New York in September 1908. One may reasonably assume that the purpose of Kern's visit to London in 1908 was partly to work closely with Grossmith on preparing the piece, and doubtless it was mainly during this London visit that Kern spent much time at Grossmith's home (see p. 18). It would seem that Kern was working on his contributions to *Fluffy Ruffles* with Bovill in London while his co-composer, William T. Francis, was working in America with the show's principal lyricist, Wallace Irwin, on the rest of the show. And, since Kern seems to have collaborated with Bovill at no other time, one may hazard a guess that the undated "Steady Little Girlie" referred to by Bordman[77] as among Kern's surviving manuscripts also dates from 1908. It may well have been intended for *Fluffy Ruffles* and replaced in New York by "Sweetest Girl, Silly Boy, I Love You," Kern's sole collaboration with Irwin.

Grossmith refers briefly in his autobiography to his experiences in *Fluffy Ruffles*.[78] He tells of how he planned to introduce into the show the "Apache Dance," to music by Offenbach, that had recently created a sensation for Max Déarly and Mistinguette at the Moulin Rouge in Paris, and which Kern was later to use in the Trocadero scene of *Show Boat*. In the end the idea of using it in *Fluffy Ruffles* was abandoned, and at the last minute Grossmith was given a new song to sing, with which he was clearly not impressed:

> It was a pointless song with a poor tune, and never received two hands of approval at any performance. I sought Mr. Frohman and begged him to take it out. "No one likes it," I protested.
>
> "*I* like it," he decided, and there the matter remained.

Whether it was one of Kern's songs Grossmith does not say.

Kern's return home from England in 1908 may have been accelerated by the progress of his father's final illness. However, his grieving over his father's death (on 13 August 1908) would have been eased by the final rehearsals for the New York productions of *The Girls of Gottenberg* and *Fluffy Ruffles*. Whenever he did return to New York from London that year he would have done so with a clutch of songs ready for publication. When proof copies began to cross the Atlantic from Harms, however, it was no longer through Ascherberg, Hopwood & Crew that they went for British copyright registration: all the deposits made in London between August and October 1908 were in the name of Jerome D. Kern himself. And on each of the proof copies deposited at the British Library there is a typewritten sticker showing, after Kern's name, the address "44 Hamlet Gardens Mansions, Ravenscourt Park."

Hamlet Gardens Mansions is still standing today, a large five-story apartment block in typical late-Victorian red brick, built in 1898 on the site of the Hamlet House Estate in Ravenscourt Park, at that time an elegant part of the Hammersmith district of West London. Whether Kern actually lived there, or whether it was merely an accommodation address, is unclear. Certainly it seems likely that Kern would have been in New York rather than London when the actual London copyright deposits showing the address were made, in August, September, and October 1908.

The Hammersmith rating records reveal that the tenant of 44 Hamlet Gardens Mansions in 1908—but not in 1907 or 1909—was one William Francis. The immediate assumption might be that this was the William T. Francis who was General Director of Charles Frohman's Musical Comedy Enterprises and the principal composer of *Fluffy Ruffles*. Certainly that William T. Francis had been in London in 1907 conducting Ivan Caryll's *Nelly Neil* for Frohman, and moreover it was not merely Kern's songs for *Fluffy Ruffles* that were copyrighted in London in Kern's name with the Hammersmith address but those of Francis too. Perhaps more likely, however, is the suggestion that the William Francis who was the tenant of 44 Hamlet Gardens Mansions was William Francis, Jr., of Francis, Day & Hunter, who had gone to New York in 1905 to help set up the firm's New York office but had returned to London in 1906 during his father's final illness.[79] Yet even this deduction must carry some doubt, since the *Post Office London Street Directory* adds to the confusion by naming the occupant of 44 Hamlet Gardens Mansions in 1908 as Edwin, rather than William, Francis—a name not to be found among the many sons of William Francis, Sr., who had attended his funeral in January 1908.[80] The main reason for believing that 44 Hamlet Gardens Mansions represented an accommodation address for Francis, Day & Hunter is that many of the song copies in the British Library deposited for copyright in Kern's name during 1908 had evidently had on them a Francis, Day & Hunter rubber stamp which was laboriously (but incompletely) scratched out and the Kern copyright claim and typewritten address-sticker superimposed. Moreover, a copy of the song "Frieda," with Kern's copyright claim and typewritten address, is still to be found in the Francis, Day & Hunter files now at EMI Music Publishing.

What is the explanation for this apparently surreptitious dealing by Kern with a firm that was ostensibly a rival to his own firm's London agent? In fact the renewed contact between Kern, Harms, and Francis, Day & Hunter is readily explained. In *The Story of Francis, Day & Hunter* John Abbott describes how the American music industry was facing lean times and having to cut overheads drastically.[81] Thus in 1908 it was decided to merge the American branch of Francis, Day & Hunter with T. B. Harms to form T. B. Harms & Francis, Day & Hunter. The copyright deposits in Kern's name were evidently part of the means of dealing with the complications that arose in respect of Harms's London representation. Once again, therefore, an extended Kern visit to London may be seen as being associated with a change in Harms's London representation and the need for Kern to carry out business for his employer, as well as to pursue the interests of his own career as a composer.

7

LITTLE EVA

With Harms once again associated with Francis, Day & Hunter, the American firm's relationship with Ascherberg, Hopwood & Crew was something of an anomaly. For a time Harms did, however, remain their U.S. agent, and, by way of reciprocal business, a few Harms songs were sent over to Ascherberg, Hopwood & Crew for copyright registration even after they began in 1909 to appear under the T. B. Harms & Francis, Day & Hunter imprint. By 1910, however, the link between Harms and Ascherberg, Hopwood & Crew had finally been severed, as the London firm acquired a new U.S. agent in Edward Schuberth & Co., which in turn was replaced in 1911 by Leo Feist, Inc.

It may well have been this final unscrambling of links with Ascherberg, Hopwood & Crew, or some other Harms business, that brought Kern back to London again in 1909. At all events it would have been then that he collaborated with Adrian Ross and George Grossmith on numbers for Leo Fall's *The Dollar Princess*, in its American production. Bordman seems to be mistaken in suggesting that "A Boat Sails on Wednesday" and "Red, White and Blue" were written for the British production:[82] the latter seems never to have been deposited for copyright registration in Britain, and the stock book of Ascherberg, Hopwood & Crew, who handled the former, quite specifically refers to it as being for the American version of the operetta. Bordman is also mistaken in suggesting that the almost simultaneous production of *The Dollar Princess* in New York and London in September 1909 testified to "the excellence and efficiency of Frohman's producing organization."[83] In fact the London production was under the George Edwardes banner and had nothing to do with Frohman. Moreover, the show had been mounted in Manchester as early as December 1908 and had then been confined to the provinces because of the continuing success of *The Merry Widow* at Daly's. Between Manchester and London the show underwent considerable rewriting, including the addition of a wholly new comedy role for W. H. Berry. It may be that Kern saw the work in the provinces and did his writing for the American production while the British lyricist, Adrian

Ross, was reworking it for London. In his expert study *Operetta: A Theatrical History* Richard Traubner astutely points to the similarities between Kern and Leo Fall, the original composer of *The Dollar Princess*, in their ability to spin a light, airy melody with a conversational turn of phrase that was some way removed from the typical rum-tum-tum of much Viennese operetta of the time.[84] It may be that in 1909 Kern met, or at any rate acquired an admiration for the work of, Fall, who also appears to have been directly involved in the changes that were made to *The Dollar Princess* between Manchester and London. (The published edition of the vocal score corresponding to the Manchester production has additional numbers by Leo Fall's brother Richard, while that corresponding to the London version has replacement numbers by Leo Fall himself.)

On his 1909 visit Kern would also have had further British shows with which to catch up. From George Edwardes there was *Our Miss Gibbs* at the Gaiety and *The Arcadians* at the Shaftesbury, and from Frank Curzon *King of Cadonia* at the Prince of Wales'. Once again Kern's particular interest would have centered upon the Frohman production at the Hicks Theatre, which was *The Dashing Little Duke*, a period-costume piece starring the Hickses, for which Frank Tours had composed his first full-length West End score. Kern's artistic contacts were gathered together in some force on 29 April, when his favored American interpreter Julia Sanderson was added to the cast. And with her were added three Kern songs.[85] Unfortunately the press report provides no clue to their identity, and it may be that they were songs that Julia Sanderson had already sung in America, either in *The Dairymaids* or in *Kitty Grey*.

Seemingly, though, the business motivation for the 1909 visit was relatively slight and the songs Kern wrote relatively few. Perhaps his stay also was brief. Or perhaps he was simply too busy with affairs of the heart. After all, he had by this time met his future wife, Eva Leale, at the riverside Swan Hotel in Manor Road, Walton-on-Thames, where her father, George Leale, was manager.

The Swan is still, today, a busy public house, imposingly situated with a garden leading down to the Thames. But the role that both the hotel and the river played in everyday life was very different in Edwardian times. One who knew both well before the First World War is Louise Bale, who moved into the Swan when her father took over from George Leale in 1911 and who, at the age of 96, still lives in nearby Weybridge. She recalls "a lovely peaceful river in those days . . . , lovely meadows with alder trees dipping down into the water, which made ideal places for courting couples to tie up their punts and dinghys in the evenings."[86] She goes on:

At weekends people came down from London, some to stay in their camps and bungalows on Tumbling Bay Island and some at the Swan. They wore pretty muslin and voile summer dresses and wide brimmed summer hats and parasols. The men wore cream flannel trousers and cable stitched sweaters and navy blazers and straw boaters, all looking very smart. When not wearing their blazers the sweaters were tied round their waists or shoulders. The river was very good for punts in the Walton reach, very shallow. . . .

Besides the pleasure boats plying the river, Miss Bale recalls that local barges came to Walton Wharf almost daily with coal for the gasworks in Manor Road, and a horse and cart went up and down the hill beside the hotel, starting about 7:30 a.m., to take the coal to the works. She also recalls that London clubs used to hold their swimming galas nearby, with tea at the Swan afterwards. The local angling club, too, was based at the Swan, and every summer Walton had a town regatta, with fireworks across the river and tea served on the lawn of the Swan. The Swan provided bed and breakfast (with a special bedroom for honeymoon couples), lunches, dinners, and teas. "There were various bars," Miss Bale recalls:

> The Tap Room had a table for crib and dominoes and shove-halfpenny, [and] darts. There was sawdust on the floor, [and] also spittoons for customers to spit into – a "must" in those days. Then there was a public bar, a private bar and a lounge – this for all classes of people. . . . Also actors came down from London now and again, and some from America. They all made the Swan their local. . . .

Precisely in which year Kern first arrived at the Swan is one of the matters about which his biographers disagree. David Ewen states that it was in 1908,[87] Gerald Bordman that it was in 1909.[88] Both agree that it was in the company of the actor James Blakeley, who lived near by. Bordman adds that Kern had gone with Lauri de Frece and Tom Reynolds to the Walton area to spend a few days on Tumbling Bay Island.[89] The fact that Blakeley was in America from 1906 to 1909, touring in *The Little Cherub* and *The Girls of Gottenberg*, might seem to argue in favor of the later date, but one clearly cannot rule out the likelihood that Blakeley would have returned home to England for a holiday at some time during that period. The information that Eva was seventeen when she first met Kern[90] would be consistent with it having been either 1908 or 1909. Perhaps it is impossible to resolve the matter now.

On one other point of debate Bordman is undoubtedly correct.[91] In describing Eva Leale's background he refers to Kern's daughter disputing the evidence of her mother's birth certificate as to her place of birth. According to the daughter, Eva Leale was born in Farringdon Street, London. However, the annual *Post Office*

London Street Directory for the years 1887 to 1897 shows George Draper Leale, beer retailer, as the occupant of 98 Cornwall Road, Lambeth; only in the 1895 to 1898 editions is he shown as being at the Crown & Anchor public house, 28 Farringdon Street. (Thus for the three years 1895-97 he was listed at both addresses.) Evidently Eva Leale was born in Lambeth and moved across the river at the age of three or so.

In reflecting upon the transatlantic romance of Kern and Eva Leale, one small piece of speculation may be worth airing. In his youthful days Kern had written music for a production of *Uncle Tom's Cabin;* in 1907 he had returned to the same source for a song "Little Eva" sung in *The Dairymaids.* What, one may wonder, was the extent of Kern's interest in Harriet Beecher Stowe's story? Had it, perhaps, come to mean so much to him that it helped him fall in love—at first sight, we are told—when he came upon a real-life "Little Eva" at the Swan, Walton-on-Thames?

Before Kern returned to England once more and married Eva in 1910, he had begun one further collaboration with a British lyricist. On this occasion, however, the collaboration would seem to have taken place not in London but in New York, since the lyricist was Frederick Day, son of the co-founder of Francis, Day & Hunter and the man who had been in charge of the firm's New York office since 1905.[92] Together he and Kern worked on songs for *Our Miss Gibbs* and *The Hen Pecks* in 1910 and *La Belle Paree* in 1911, before Day returned to London in the latter year. In 1956, by which time he had become Chairman of Francis, Day & Hunter, Fred Day published a selection of his lyrics in book form under the name of Edward Montagu (apparently his middle Christian names and adopted as a *nom de plume* for his later lyrics). Among the lyrics included are two for music by Kern.[93] One is "The Manicure Girl" from *The Hen Pecks;* the other, "Isn't It Nice to Have Somebody 'Crazy' About You?" from an unnamed show, is not to be found among the recognized titles of Kern songs. However, it is clear from the words and layout that this is the concerted piece "Betty's Advice," which is listed among published items from *Our Miss Gibbs* on copyright deposits but appears to be missing from major Kern song collections. As regards another Day/Kern song from *Our Miss Gibbs* for which Bordman apparently searched in vain,[94] "I Don't Want You to Be a Sister to Me," proof copies are to be found both in the British Library and in the Francis, Day & Hunter files at EMI Music Publishing.

Kern's visit to Britain in 1910 had no obvious business connotations. It seems to have been purely for personal reasons, and the only evidence we have for it is the knowledge that on 25 October 1910 he married Eva Leale at St. Mary's Church,

Walton-on-Thames. Long-time residents of Walton recalled that Kern had appeared in the town in August that year, and it seems that, for a short time following their marriage, he and Eva lived at 76 Manor Road, close to the Swan.[95] David Ewen tells us that they spent their honeymoon in London and visited the White City,[96] which would have been for the Japan-British Exhibition which closed on 29 October. Then they left for their new home in the U.S.A. Thus ended the youthful visits of Kern to London in the year that symbolically also saw the death of King Edward VII and brought to a close the brief but glamorous reign in which British musical comedy had flourished as never before or since.

During the previous five and a half years Jerome Kern must have felt almost as much at home in London as in New York. The evidence assembled here suggests that he made at least five separate visits to London—in mid-1905, early 1906, early 1908, mid-1909, and late 1910. Some of these periods may have included more than one trip, of course, and there may have been other visits of which no trace has been uncovered. On any count, the visits were a significant experience for the young man in his early twenties: they gave him an abiding love of Britain and provided him with experience and contacts that were to prove invaluable both for his own career and for the evolution and establishment of the American musical.

8

LONDON LEGACY

It is, in its way, ironic that the tying of the knot between Jerome Kern and Eva Leale should have been the signal not for Kern to increase his visits to Britain but to reduce them. He and Eva may well have made some private return visit in the early years of their marriage, but it seems to have been as much as eleven years before Kern was to make a further business trip across the Atlantic.

Clearly the war clouds that were soon to gather over Europe were a factor in extending the duration of this absence. Eva Leale's love of the U.S.A. must have been another factor that kept Kern away from Britain. Yet there were clearly other significant business reasons. Most immediately, perhaps, was the fact that with T. B. Harms now firmly wedded to Francis, Day & Hunter there was no longer a need for renewed negotiations with London agents. There was also the fact that London could no longer be considered the same force in the international musical theater that it had been. At the Gaiety, for instance, the creative partnership that had lasted for fifteen years between Ivan Caryll and Lionel Monckton had broken up after *Our Miss Gibbs*. At around the same time the failure of *The Dashing Little Duke* had brought the productions of the Hickses to an end in financial disaster, and with it the substantial interest of Charles Frohman in the London musical theater. Now Viennese operetta was in the ascendant, and Frohman seems to have been inclined to go direct to Vienna for his new shows. Thus there were no longer the same reasons for Kern to visit London, especially as he was now kept fully occupied at home, with the U.S.A. increasingly an exporter rather than an importer of song material.

Moreover, Eva Leale's connections with her former life in Walton-on-Thames were progressively reduced from within a year of Eva's and Jerry's departure for the U.S.A. In 1911 George Leale retired from the Swan to live in a house in Manor Road, and the recently married couple's account of their life in America may have persuaded Eva's younger brother and sister to make adventurous plans for the future. Apparently both Ethel and Albert Leale soon followed their elder sister to America.[97]

Bordman suggests that the Kerns may also have made a visit to Europe in 1914,[98] citing Kern's being listed in ASCAP's records as the composer of a song called "Die süsse Pariserin" for a German show called *Die Ballkönigin*. Actually the song title was copyrighted in 1913, and Bordman evidently failed to uncover the fact that *Die Ballkönigin*, produced in Vienna in July 1913, was a German version of the 1904 Charles Frohman/Seymour Hicks musical *The Catch of the Season*.[99] Just what the Kern song that went with the work to Vienna might have been is unclear, though the German title (which means "The Sweet Parisian Girl") might make one think of "Rosalie," whose lyric runs: "Rosalie, Rosalie, très jolie, Rosalie,/Truly all Paris worships you, ma mie." Whatever the song may have been, there is nothing particularly surprising in one of Kern's songs going with the show to Vienna, and absolutely no reason why it should have involved Kern and his wife in a trip to Germany. Likewise one may reasonably discount the idea that the inclusion of songs by Kern in wartime London shows would have involved further trips by him to Britain. In *Rosy Rapture, the Pride of the Beauty Chorus*, produced at Frohman's Duke of York's Theatre in 1915, for instance, Kern's "Best Sort of Mother, Best Sort of Child" was indeed, as Bordman surmises, the song "Same Sort of Girl" with a different lyric.[100] With London demonstrating an ever increasing appetite for American popular song, Kern's American hits were by then beginning to appear with some regularity in London musical comedies and revues.

Yet, if both Kern and the Harms firm were able to flourish without any need for his renewed presence in London, there is not a shadow of doubt that the progress of Kern's career was now being aided by the contacts he had made in Edwardian London. Time and again his name was associated with men he had met in those early visits. Thus in New York in 1911, for instance, what Bordman rightly describes as Kern's "biggest opportunity since *Mr. Wix of Wickham*"[101] saw him once again sharing the composer credits with Frank Tours for *La Belle Paree*. When one of the show's songs, "The Human Brush," came to London in 1912, it was in an Empire Theatre revue, *All the Winners*, written by Kern's old collaborator C. H. Bovill, who also revised the lyric of Kern's song for London.

It is in the performance of Kern's songs in Britain that we particularly find the names of his faithful friends and supporters recurring. Connections with Alfred Butt and the Palace Theatre, for instance, were revived in 1914 when Kern's "You're Here

Jerome Kern as a young man:
portrait inscribed "To Eva with Love from Jerry"
(courtesy Mrs. Betty Kern Miller)

The Gaiety Theatre at the time of *The Spring Chicken* (1905–6)
(author's collection)

Seymour Hicks in *The Beauty of Bath*,
from *The Play Pictorial*, no. 45 (1906) (author's collection)

THE FROLIC OF THE BREEZE.

The Names of the
ladies are the Misses—

STANDEN, LESLIE,
CARTER, DAVISON,
STOREY, JAMES,
BORELLI, BATEMAN
and LAWS.

A STEAMSHIP rolled in the river cold,
    And it didn't seem to know which way to go.
It was drawing near to bump the pier
    When suddenly the breeze began to blow :
The vessel heeled, a passenger reeled,
    And fell into the water on the spot.
"Hi, save that man," yelled the skipper,
    "If you can.
He's the only blooming passenger we've got !"

Oh, wee up ! the wayward wind was blowing,
    And the weather looked like snowing,
And the water was at forty-two degrees,
    But he answered, with a shiver,
    "I feel safer in the river,
Than aboard a penny steamer in the breeze,
On a County Council Steamer in the breeze."

Tattersall Spink—MR. BERT SINDEN.

"The Frolic of a Breeze" (*The Beauty of Bath*),
from *The Play Pictorial*, no. 45 (1906) (author's collection)

Frank Tours: caricature by Lawrence Grossmith (photo: Dover Street Studios), from *The Tatler*, 18 April 1906 (courtesy the British Library)

Street Hawker (crying his songs):
"''OW'D YER LIKE TO SPOON WID ME?'
'IN THE SHADE O' THE OLE APPLE TREE.'"

Popular song titles in incongruous settings,
cartoon from *Cassell's Magazine*, February 1907 (author's collection)

George Grossmith, Jr.
(photo: Ellis & Walery) (author's collection)

Millie Legarde singing "How'd You Like to Spoon With Me?"
Palace Theatre, 12 February 1906 (photo: Campbell-Gray),
from *The Sketch*, 21 February 1906 (courtesy the British Library)

The Gay Lothario

Words by C. H. BOVILL   Music by JEROME D. KERN

Sung by Mr. GEORGE GROSSMITH, Junr.

"The Gay Lothario" (*A Waltz Dream*),
from *The Play Pictorial*, no. 57 (1908)
(author's collection; courtesy T. B. Harms Co.)

The river entrance to the Swan Hotel, Walton-on-Thames, *ca* 1910 (courtesy Weybridge Museum)

The Swan Hotel, *ca* 1910 (courtesy Weybridge Museum)

St. Mary's Church, Walton-on-Thames, *ca* 1910 (courtesy Weybridge Museum)

and I'm Here" was included in the revue *The Passing Show*, and again in 1916 when "Some Sort of Somebody" turned up in the revue *Vanity Fair*. Both were orchestrated for the Palace Theatre by the long-serving musical director Herman Finck, who had done the same for "How'd You Like to Spoon With Me?" back in 1906.[102] Butt also took over the Adelphi Theatre after George Edwardes's death in October 1915, and there in 1916 another of Kern's Edwardian associates, W. H. Berry, star of *Venus, 1906*, sang the Kern song "It Isn't My Fault" in *High Jinks*. Butt's next show at the Adelphi Theatre, *The Boy*, included yet another song by Kern, "Have a Heart!"

The other name that crops up time and again in connection with the introduction of Kern's music into Britain is that of George Grossmith. His contribution to Kern's gaining a foothold in Britain during the Edwardian era has already been highlighted. If this allegiance may have faded somewhat when Kern went back to America, it did so only temporarily. When the outbreak of war closed the London theaters in 1914, Grossmith went to the U.S.A. with the Gaiety Theatre company as star of the musical *To-Night's the Night*. While there the company, which also included Kern's old friend James Blakeley, attended the first-night party for Kern's *Ninety in the Shade*, at which Guy Bolton and P. G. Wodehouse most probably first met.[103] When *To-Night's the Night* returned home to the reopened Gaiety Theatre in May 1915 it included two songs by Kern sung by Grossmith himself—"They Didn't Believe Me" and "Any Old Night." (The latter had only recently been heard in New York, in *Nobody Home*, the Princess Theatre version of the old Paul Rubens work *Mr. Popple (of Ippleton)* in which George Grossmith's brother Lawrence was now playing the role of Mr. Popple. "They Didn't Believe Me" soon became a favorite in Britain and was transported, by soldiers returning from leave, across the Channel to the battlefields of Europe.) Then in 1916, when Ivor Novello had difficulty in delivering the score for the musical *Theodore & Co.*, written and produced by Grossmith for the Gaiety Theatre, Grossmith again turned to Kern, who responded with a handful of songs which were adapted by Grossmith's new lyricist Clifford Grey for a show that saw Kern receive his first London billing as joint composer.

It was at Alfred Butt's Palace Theatre, once again, that Kern's name appeared in London for the first time as a show's principal composer, with *Very Good Eddie* in 1918. Some of Kern's original songs were replaced in London by those of other composers; but then some reconstruction of Kern's score had been made inevitable by the fact that two of its numbers had already been used in London—"Some Sort of Somebody" in *Vanity Fair* and "Isn't It Great to be Happily Married" (as "Can't

You See I Mean You?" alias "All That I Want Is Somebody to Love Me") in *Theodore & Co.*[104]

Once again, however, Butt's contribution to Kern's growing fame in London was trumped by Grossmith, who, with his production partner Edward Laurillard, produced *Oh, Boy!* (under the slightly altered title *Oh, Joy!*) at the Kingsway Theatre in 1919. Grossmith's greatest service to Kern, however, perhaps lay in the series of productions that he and Laurillard put on at the Winter Garden Theatre between 1921 and 1923. The first was of *Sally*, which did so much for American musical-comedy song on both sides of the Atlantic. The second and third were of *The Cabaret Girl* and *The Beauty Prize*—shows commissioned expressly for the Winter Garden by Grossmith, who not only appeared in them but provided the lyrics, in partnership with P. G. Wodehouse.

It was for *Sally* in 1921 that Jerry and Eva Kern returned to London for what Grossmith confirms as their first visit since before the War. Kern was delighted to be back in London, according to Grossmith, who quotes him as follows: "It's just wonderful to be here again. It's the only place in the world. I have just one more play to do for Dillingham, then I'm going to wind up my affairs in New York and settle here for ever."[105] How much truth there is in this quotation we cannot know, but Kern's abiding love for London is certainly not to be doubted. (As Grossmith also confirms, however, it was not shared by his wife, who could not wait to get back to the life they had made for themselves in Bronxville, New York.)

It was the two years and more when Kern's shows held the stage at the Winter Garden that signaled quite definitely the acceptance of American musical comedy in Britain. They led to the almost automatic production in Britain of subsequent successes, not only by Kern himself but by the Gershwins, Youmans, Rodgers and Hart, and others. Thus by 1926 *Sunny* was able to enjoy a good run at the Hippodrome without, for once, any obvious involvement of the contacts of Kern's youth.

Sunny's producer, Lee Ephraim, was soon to demonstrate his own allegiance to Kern, however, by commissioning a score for the newly opened Piccadilly Theatre in 1928. For this Kern came once more to London. In *Blue Eyes* he was reintroduced to the Scottish milieu that he had attempted to evoke years ago in his Frohman test piece "The Bagpipe Serenade," and he was associated once again with W. H. Berry, as well as with Frank Tours, who composed an interpolated number, "Women," for Berry.

The 1928 visit also provided some other, significant displays of loyalty from the contacts of Kern's early days in London. For Grossmith's latest vehicle, *Lady Mary*, Kern allowed his 1924 song "In Love With Love" to be fitted with a revised lyric by Graham John as "If You're a Friend of Mine." (The principal composer of *Lady Mary*, Albert Sirmay, was apparently already installed as music editor at Chappell-Harms.) But the other principal purpose of the 1928 visit was for Kern to supervise the London production of *Show Boat*, which Alfred Butt was producing at the Drury Lane Theatre, where the musical director was again his old Palace Theatre associate, Herman Finck. Kern had provided one wholly new song, "Dance Away the Night," for the London production; he also permitted one other addition, which in the context of this study is far more interesting. In the Trocadero scene in Act 2, in place of the duet "Good-bye, My Lady Love," was introduced his old success "How'd You Like to Spoon With Me?"[106] (It is to be found there in the libretto published by Chappell.) As a period vaudeville-style piece its use there was, of course, entirely appropriate. Yet for the show's composer (Kern), producer (Butt), and conductor (Finck) it must have meant far more, as a nostalgic reminder of the three's combining to introduce the song to London at the Palace Theatre more than twenty-two years before.

In the early 1930s Kern's music held sway in London through Charles B. Cochran's productions of *The Cat and the Fiddle* at the Palace in 1932 and *Music in the Air* at His Majesty's the following year. It was also at His Majesty's that the last show written by Kern for London, *Three Sisters*, was produced in 1934. Again there were no obvious links with his youthful days in London, and indeed many of Kern's associates of that time were by now dead or retired. The show itself was not a success, but it did produce one lasting standard in "I Won't Dance." In truth, the song made no particular mark in *Three Sisters*; it achieved immortality only when finding its definitive place in the film of *Roberta*—a vivid demonstration of the way in which popular music's dissemination was changing.

Film songs were to occupy the bulk of Kern's compositional time from then on. Yet, even in this final stage of his career, when he was writing sophisticated songs far removed from those of his youth, he permitted himself one last, remarkable backward glimpse at his days in London—thousands of miles and now nearly 40 years away. In *Cover Girl* in 1944 he included in the score a song, sung by Nan Wynn as the voice of Rita Hayworth, that was not by himself; it was the old British music-hall song "Poor John!" Again, as with "How'd You Like to Spoon With Me?" in *Show Boat*, it was entirely appropriate to its setting. But, whereas for many millions of the film's viewers it was just an old music-hall song, for Kern it must have been something more. The song had been introduced in Britain in the very year of his first successes there, 1906, by Vesta Victoria, who later had a success with it in America. Most particularly Kern's memories must have been of the Francis, Day & Hunter premises in Charing Cross Road, to which he would have made the first visit of his 1905 trip—for the words of "Poor John!" were by Francis, Day & Hunter's literary editor at the time, Kern's collaborator Fred W. Leigh, and the music by the firm's music editor, Henry E. Pether.

9

CODA

During the first half of the twentieth century the world changed enormously—socially, politically, and musically. Popular music, not least, changed vastly from the days when Kern passed those many youthful months in London: in the early 1900s the regular beat and fluent melodies of European popular music had ruled the roost, whereas by the 1940s it was the brasher, rhythmically freer, vernacularly shaped phrases of American popular song that held sway. Kern had been in the forefront of that revolution, and the days he spent in London in his youth had played no small part in bringing this about. To Kern himself they were of considerable personal importance for giving him an entree to the musical theater not only in London but also (through his contract with Frohman) in New York. But in terms of the whole development of the American popular musical theater, too, their significance should not be overlooked.

How much longer might the American musical have taken to penetrate the London theater if Kern had not made those contacts in 1905 and 1906? How much longer might the American musical have had to wait for acceptance in Europe if it had not been for Kern's association with George Grossmith and the latter's productions of *Oh, Boy!*, *Sally*, *The Cabaret Girl*, and *The Beauty Prize*? How much longer might it have taken for American popular song to gain worldwide acceptance if "They Didn't Believe Me" had not been so speedily transported across the Atlantic by Grossmith to the Gaiety, and thence across the Channel to the battlefields of Europe?

Perhaps such changes would not have been long delayed. Yet Kern was able to help ensure that the transition in popular musical styles was brought about speedily and efficiently. In his youth he had gained an intimate knowledge of European popular musical styles at their source, and like all revolutionaries he was able to bring about the transition all the more readily by having established a position within the establishment he was ultimately to help overturn.

APPENDIX 1: SOME SONG PUZZLES INVESTIGATED

It is perhaps worth taking the time and space to consider points about certain songs that have been raised by Bordman and other writers that do not relate particularly to Kern's youthful visits to London but about which British sources provide some illumination.

"How'd You Like to Spoon With Me?"

In his article in *Variety* on "How'd You Like to Spoon With Me?,"[107] Edward Laska, its lyricist, recalled that the song had been turned down in New York by Charles Frohman's general manager Alf Hayman on the grounds that the word "spoon" was "entirely unknown" in England. But was this in fact the case? If so, it is surprising that, considering the adaptation of American lyrics for British consumption that was commonplace at that time, this song was published in Britain virtually unchanged.

In fact the suggestion that "spoon" was unknown in Britain cannot have been correct. It was apparently quite common in late-Victorian and Edwardian plays and popular songs. Around 1870, for instance, the term had been used prominently in a British music-hall song entitled "Spooning on the Sands" (words by Frank W. Green, music by Alfred Lee).[108] Then again, in William Fullerton's comic opera *The Lady of the Locket* (words by H. H. Hamilton; 1885) there occurs a song that runs:

> There once was a gay young coster bloke,
> There once was a belted Earl,
> Who both, at an inauspicious stroke,
> Got spoons on the self-same girl. . . .[109]

And at around the very time that Alf Hayman was supposedly making his statement, London was enjoying the musical comedy *The Earl and the Girl*, into which had been interpolated the American song "My Cosey Corner Girl" (words by Charles Noel Douglas, music by John W. Bratton), which includes the line "But when I spoon I want no moon."

So the word "spoon" was certainly not unknown in Britain. But one appearance of the term in popular song in Britain seems of especial interest in relation to the reception of Jerome Kern's first hit song in London. The song in question is known in America as "Down Where the Wurzburger Flows," one of a series of beer-drinking songs composed by Harry von Tilzer, with words by Vincent P. Bryan. It was copyrighted in London in its American edition in May 1902 and then, despite the seeming incomprehensibility of its lyric for British audiences, published by Francis, Day & Hunter in a British edition with unchanged lyric in September 1903. Notwithstanding its catchy tune, it not surprisingly seems to have made little impact. Then early in 1905, perhaps encouraged by the way in which another of Von Tilzer's beer-drinking songs, "Under the Anheuser Busch," had been anglicized by the rival publishing house of Feldman's as "Down at the Old Bull and Bush," the earlier song was retrieved and given a new lyric by Fred W. Leigh. Although the basic idea of bringing the countryside into town was retained, there was otherwise nothing in common between Leigh's lyric and Bryan's original. Nonetheless the original lyricist was named as co-lyricist with Leigh. The song became "Riding on Top of the Car," a song in praise of the British tramcar.[110] In this form the song was copyrighted in May 1905 and introduced to the British public by a leading variety singer of the time, George Lashwood. It became a considerable hit, and Lashwood made a recording of it in July 1905.

What is relevant here is that, athough the word "spoon" is nowhere to be found in Bryan's original American lyric, it appears prominently in two places in the British lyric by Leigh. In the first two lines of the song we hear: "Some people declare that a quiet country lane/Is the very best place for a 'spoon.' " Then again, in the refrain: "The seats are so small, and there's not much to pay./You sit close together and 'spoon' all the way."

The especially intriguing aspect of this appearance of "spoon" in a British song lyric is its coinciding with the success of Kern's song. Can one possibly believe that this prominent introduction of the word into a lyric by Francis, Day & Hunter's literary editor and copyrighted in May 1905 had nothing to do with that firm's receipt of Kern's song in March 1905 for U.K. copyright deposit and possible publication? And after Kern's song the term became something of a staple of song lyrics. It appeared prominently, for instance, in his own song "Ballooning" (1907), whose style and content Bordman suggests may have been intended specifically to capitalize on the popularity of "How'd You Like to Spoon With Me?"[111] Perhaps significantly, this was one of the few Kern songs of the time to be published in Britain. The term's use by other songwriters as a rhyme for "moon" may be highlighted by two other successes on either side of the Atlantic in 1909—the American "By the Light of the Silvery Moon" (words by Edward Madden, music by Gus Edwards) and the British "I Used to Sigh for the Silvery Moon" (words by Lester Barrett, music by Herman Darewski).

"Missing" Songs

As has been shown, the copies of Kern's songs deposited for copyright in London at the time of original publication help to fill in some of the gaps in Bordman's coverage. "A Plain Rustic Ride" in *The Little Cherub* and "I Don't Want You to Be a Sister to Me" in *Our Miss Gibbs* have already been cited; another is the march "Farewell, Dear Toys" written for *The Babes and the Baron* of December 1905.[112] During 1909 and 1910, however, the depositing of Kern's songs in Britain became curiously intermittent—perhaps because of the complicated relationship between Harms and Ascherberg, Hopwood & Crew. Thus the British Library collection sheds no light on two further songs that Bordman was unable to trace, "Eulalie" from *Kitty Grey* and "Shine Out, All You Little Stars" from *The Gay Hussars*.[113] However, copies of these and other "missing" songs are in the collections of James J. Fuld of New York and (according to the *National Union Catalog*) the University of California, Berkeley. Other important bodies of Kern songs are in the collection of Lester S. Levy of Pikesville, Maryland, and the Walter Harding collection at the Bodleian Library, Oxford—both of which contain, for instance, the song "Red, White and Blue" from *The Dollar Princess*, another song that may be sought in vain in the British Library.

"Won't You Have a Little Feather?"

One song that Bordman mentions in passing is "Won't You Have a Little Feather?"[114] He connects it only with Charles Dillingham's 1924 revival of *Peter Pan*. The London copyright deposit edition makes it clear, however, that the song was written for Frohman's original New York production of the play. The copy deposited at the British Library in December 1907 is, unusually, a finished edition, which is consistent with the printed edition's having been prepared somewhat earlier. That the lyricist was Paul West, with whom Kern otherwise worked only on songs copyrighted between October 1906 and May 1907, suggests that the *Peter Pan* song also derives from this period. In all probability it was intended for Frohman's production during the 1906-7 season but not used.

"My Otaheitee Lady"

Another point in Bordman's biography worth straightening out concerns the song "My Otaheitee Lady," which Kern provided for Arthur Wing Pinero's play *The Amazons* in 1913. Bordman asserts that this must have been a song that Kern salvaged from his high school show—apparently on the grounds of a 1902 copyright claim in the name of Francis, Day & Hunter.[115] Yet Kern had nothing to do with the London firm as early as 1902, and the song was actually copyrighted in Kern's name only in 1913. This should be enough to make it clear that the link with Kern's early days assumed by Bordman is fallacious. The 1902 copyright date relates merely to the lyric (by Charles H. Taylor). In its original form this lyric was for a British song "My Otaheite [*sic*] Lady,"[116] composed by John Neat and Herbert E. Haines and sung by the variety artist Ada Reeve:

> My Otaheite lady
> I still can see her smile
> Where the palms grow green and shady
> On a South Pacific isle.
> I still can hear her call me
> Her dandy ocean swell,
> Oh! my Otaheite, Otaheite,
> Otaheite belle!

Perhaps Kern knew the song from his London days and felt that the lyric fitted a situation in *The Amazons*. In adapting Taylor's verses, he altered the meter here and there by expanding certain phrases, and also turned Taylor's third person singular into the second person singular.

"Do I Do Wrong?"

In his discussion of *Blue Eyes* Bordman debates when the song "Do I Do Wrong?" (later transformed into "You're Devastating" in *Roberta)* was added to the score.[117] Further evidence on this is provided by the publication and recording of numbers from the show.

"Do I Do Wrong?" was not among the first set of four numbers ("Bow Belles" copyrighted on 18 April 1928; "Blue Eyes," "Back to the Heather," and "Henry" copyrighted on 24 April 1928) that were evidently prepared for publication before the London opening of *Blue Eyes.* Nor is it one of the further two numbers ("In Love" and "No One Else But You") copyrighted on 15 May 1928 and issued with a new title page, evidently in conjunction with the London run. Most significantly, the pianoforte selection, apparently published at the same time as the latter two numbers, contains neither "Henry" (which had been dropped in the pre-London run) nor "Do I Do Wrong?"; evidently it had not yet been added. However, "Do I Do Wrong?" was one of the four numbers from the show that were recorded on 29 May 1928.[118] Moreover, the orchestral selection recorded on 31 May 1928 contained "Do I Do Wrong?" but not "No One Else But You," further confirming that the former had by then replaced the latter. The sheet music of "Do I Do Wrong?" was finally deposited for copyright on 7 June 1928. Hence it seems clear that the song was added sometime during May 1928, perhaps two or three weeks after the London first night.

Incidentally, Bordman suggests that the published score of *Blue Eyes* appeared "several weeks" after the opening.[119] In fact, it was as much as two years after. Since the show had by then closed, the purpose of publication must presumably have been to make the show available for amateur production. This would have meant that the published score would not necessarily have adhered totally to the form of the work as established at the Piccadilly Theatre, as Bordman seems to assume.

NOTES (to Preface, Chapters 1 to 9, and Appendix 1)

[1] Gerald Bordman, *Jerome Kern: His Life and Music* (New York and Oxford: Oxford University Press, 1980).

[2] Bordman, pp. 18-19.

[3] Bordman, pp. 19-22.

[4] David Ewen, *The Story of Jerome Kern* (New York: Henry Holt, 1953), pp. 26, 37.

[5] Ewen, *The World of Jerome Kern* (New York: Henry Holt, 1960), p. 32, and *Popular American Composers* (New York: H. W. Wilson Company, 1962), p. 101.

[6] Ewen, *The New Complete Book of the American Musical Theater* (New York: Holt, Rinehart and Winston, 1970), p. 677, and *All the Years of American Popular Music* (Englewood Cliffs: Prentice-Hall, 1977), p. 215.

[7] Bordman, p. 44.

[8] Bordman, p. 41.

[9] Bordman, pp. 33-34.

[10] Bordman, p. 33.

[11] Bordman, p. 34.

[12] Bordman, p. 41.

[13] *The Era* (17 June 1905), p. 12, col. 4.

[14] *The Era* (10 February 1906), p. 20, col. 3. "Sammy," with words by James O'Dea and music by Edward Hutchison, had just been a great success in London when interpolated into the show *The Earl and the Girl*.

[15] *The Era* (17 February 1906), p. 21, col. 1.

[16] *The Era* (3 March 1906), p. 22, col. 1.

[17] *The Sketch* (28 February 1906), p. 219; *The Tatler* (21 March 1906), p. 408.

[18] Max Wilk, *They're Playing Our Song* (New York: Atheneum, 1973), p. 17.

[19] *The Times* (20 March 1906), p. 5, col. 6.

[20] *The Stage* (22 March 1906), p. 16, col. 5.

[21] *The Era* (24 March 1906), p. 17, cols. 2-3.

[22] Bordman, p. 45.

[23] *The Times* (23 March 1906), p. 10, col. 5. (At a time when the plays, novels, and other writings of Jerome K. Jerome were greatly in vogue in Britain, the incorrect middle initial is perhaps not surprising.)

[24] *The Stage* (29 March 1906), p. 14, col. 3.

[25] *The Era* (24 March 1906), p. 17, col. 5.

[26] *The Stage* (19 April 1906), p. 18, col. 3.

[27] W. H. Berry, *Forty Years in the Limelight* (London: Hutchinson, 1939), p. 127.

[28] Bordman, p. 45.

[29] *The Stage* (10 May 1906), p. 16, col. 2. When *The Little Cherub* was produced in America later in 1906 it was essentially in this revised *Girl on the Stage* version, but under the original title.

[30] W. H. Berry describes (pp. 127-28) how he had to combine playing in *Venus, 1906* with appearing at the Prince of Wales' Theatre in *The Little Cherub/A Girl on the Stage.* In the latter he appeared only in the first and third acts, between which he had to perform his quick-change roles at the Empire. From there he emerged in his Indian regalia and rushed across Leicester Square to the Prince of Wales' Theatre, wiping off his makeup with a greased towel. His arrival at the theater was signaled by the call-boy to Frank Tours, who thereupon began the prelude to the third act while Berry changed into a toga for his next entry.

[31] John Abbott, *The Story of Francis, Day & Hunter* (London: Francis, Day & Hunter, 1952), p. 26.

[32] British Library shelf mark H.3985.

[33] For details of this and other copyright deposits, see Appendix 2.

[34] Bordman, p. 43.

[35] Reproduced in Wilk, pp. 13-16.

[36] *The Era* (22 April 1905), p. 18, col. 3.

[37] *The Era* (13 May 1905), p. 18, col. 5.

[38] *Cassell's Magazine* (February 1907), p. 397.

[39] *The Era* (22 April 1905), p. 18, col. 4.

[40] Bordman, p. 42, where the title is misquoted as "Wont You Kiss Me Once Before I Go?"

[41] *The Era* (24 June 1905), p. 18, col. 3.

[42] *The Era* (1 July 1905), p. 20, col. 5.

[43] Bordman, p. 44.

[44] Bordman, p. 34.

[45] Bordman, p. 41.

[46] Quoted by Bordman, p. 41.

[47] Bordman, pp. 42-43.

[48] George Grossmith, *"G. G."* (London: Hutchinson, 1933), pp. 30-31.

[49] Ewen, *The World of Jerome Kern*, p. 33.

[50] *Recte* "Trixie of Upper Tooting," sung in *Little Miss Nobody* in 1899, and not quite Rubens's first song sung in a London theater.

[51] Grossmith, p. 167.

[52] David A. Jasen, *P. G. Wodehouse: A Portrait of a Master*, 2nd ed. (New York: Continuum, 1981), p. 36.

[53] Ewen, *The World of Jerome Kern*, p. 33.

[54] Bertie Hollender, *Before I Forget* (London: Grayson & Grayson, 1935).

[55] Hollender, p. 51.

52

[56] Hollender, p. 51.

[57] Hollender, p. 49.

[58] Grossmith, p. 168.

[59] Bordman, p. 87.

[60] Hollender, pp. 98-100.

[61] *The Times* (8 January 1906), p. 11, col. 1.

[62] *The Times* (4 January 1906), p. 5, col. 1.

[63] Hollender, p. 51.

[64] Bordman, p. 46.

[65] Hollender, pp. 24, 37-38, 86.

[66] Hollender, p. 51.

[67] Hollender, pp. 10, 109.

[68] Hollender, p. 51.

[69] *The Sketch* (21 February 1906), p. 187.

[70] Raymond Mander & Joe Mitchenson, *British Music Hall* (London: Studio Vista, 1965), picture 221.

[71] Hollender, facing p. 258.

[72] Paul A. Rubens, "The Success of 'Mr. Popple,' " *The Tatler* (21 March 1906), p. 402.

[73] Bordman, p. 52.

[74] *The Play Pictorial*, no. 69 (Vol. 11, No. 6) (May 1908), p. 147.

[75] Bordman, p. 51.

[76] *The Stage* (7 May 1908), p. 18, col. 4.

[77] Bordman, p. 132.

[78] Grossmith, pp. 77-78.

[79] Abbott, pp. 44-45.

[80] *The Era* (18 January 1908), p. 23, col. 2.

[81] Abbott, pp. 47-48.

[82] Bordman, p. 57.

[83] Bordman, p. 57.

[84] Richard Traubner, *Operetta: A Theatrical History* (Garden City, NY: Doubleday, 1983), p. 286.

[85] *The Era* (1 May 1909), p. 16, col. 3.

[86] Louise Bale, "Life at the Swan Hotel, Walton-on-Thames, from 1911 to 1922," deposited at the Weybridge Museum.

[87] Ewen, *The World of Jerome Kern*, p. 43.

[88] Bordman, p. 56.

[89] According to Michael Freedland's *Jerome Kern: A Biography* (London: Robson Books, 1978), p. 24, the visit to the Swan was in 1909 and Kern's companion was Lawrence Grossmith, younger brother of George.

[90] Laska, quoted by Wilk, p. 15; Ewen, *The World of Jerome Kern*, p. 44.

[91] Bordman, p. 56.

[92] Abbott, pp. 43, 49.

[93] Edward Montagu, *A Hundred and One Song Lyrics* (London: Francis, Day & Hunter, 1956), pp. 98-101.

[94] Bordman, p. 62.

[95] "Town Remembers Song Man's Wife," *Surrey Herald* (10 November 1977); Morag Barton, *Victorian & Edwardian Camera Studies: Weybridge, Walton-on-Thames, Hersham, Oatlands* (Weybridge Museum, 1982).

[96] Ewen, *The World of Jerome Kern*, p. 47.

[97] *Surrey Herald* (10 November 1977).

[98] Bordman, p. 94.

[99] Anton Bauer, *Opern und Operetten in Wien* (Graz and Cologne: Hermann Böhlaus, 1955), entry 396.

[100] Bordman, p. 105. The name of the lyricist he cites, F. W. Mark, was a pseudonym for the essayist E. V. Lucas (1868-1938).

[101] Bordman, p. 63.

[102] Herman Finck, *My Melodious Memories* (London: Hutchinson, 1937), p. 177. Finck also quotes Kern's lasting fondness for the George Edwardes school of musical comedy.

[103] Bordman, p. 121.

[104] "All That I Want Is Somebody to Love Me" was the title used in the Ascherberg, Hopwood & Crew vocal score and on the original cast recording, with the lyric credited solely to Clifford Grey. However, the original American title "Can't You See I Mean You?" was used for the separate number as published by Francis, Day & Hunter, with lyric credited jointly to Grey and the original lyricist, M. E. Rourke. See Bordman, pp. 103, 130.

[105] Grossmith, p. 178.

[106] Miles Kreuger, *Show Boat: The Story of a Classic American Musical* (New York: Oxford University Press, 1977), p. 74.

[107] See above, p. 13 and note 35.

[108] Nos. 4827 and 4828 of Charles Sheard's "Musical Bouquet," British Library shelf mark H.2345.

[109] Kurt Gänzl, *The British Musical Theatre* (London: Macmillan, in preparation).

[110] British Library shelf mark H.3988.d(3).

[111] Bordman, pp. 49-50.

[112] Bordman, p. 44.

[113] Bordman, pp. 55, 58.

[114] Bordman, p. 260.

[115] Bordman, p. 81.

[116] British Library shelf mark H.3986.p(34).

[117] Bordman, p. 298.

[118] Brian Rust, *London Musical Shows on Record, 1897-1976* (Harrow: General Gramophone Publications, 1977), pp. 46, 321, 352, 460, 527.

[119] Bordman, p. 297.

APPENDIX 2: LIST OF KERN'S COMPOSITIONS, 1901–10

(Arranged by date of copyright)

Song title and lyricist	Show and principal composer (U.S. prod'n unless stated)	Publisher and copyright date*	U.K. copyright depositor & British Library shelf mark
Ma Angelina and other songs (see Bordman, pp. 18-19)	The Melodious Menu	unpublished	
various songs (see Bordman, pp. 20-22)	Uncle Tom's Cabin	unpublished	
At the Casino, Reverie (instrumental)		Lyceum 5 Sep 1902	B. Feldman h.3282.jj(58)
In a Shady Bungalow, Entr'acte [a] (instrumental)		Lyceum 5 May 1903	Price & Reynolds h.3282.jj(59)
To the End of the World Together (Edgar Smith)	An English Daisy (Slaughter)	unpublished	
Wine, Wine! (Champagne Song) [a,b] (Edgar Smith)	An English Daisy (Slaughter)	TBH 28 Dec 1903	FD & H H.3985(59)
Angling by a Babbling Brook [a,b] (Kern)	Mr. Wix of Wickham (Darnley)	TBH 16 Mar 1904	FD & H H.3985(2)
Susan [b] (Kern)	Mr. Wix of Wickham (Darnley)	TBH 30 Apr 1904	FD & H H.3985(51)
He'll Be There! [b] (J. Cheever Goodwin)		TBH 30 Apr 1904	FD & H H.3985(18)
The Downcast Eye [b] (Edgar Smith)	An English Daisy (Slaughter)	TBH 4 May 1904	FD & H H.3985(12)
My Celia [b] (words & music John L. Golden & Kern)	The Silver Slipper (Stuart)	TBH 30 Aug 1904	FD & H H.3984.d(40)

McGuire Esquire b,c (Kern)		TBH 19 Oct 1904	FD & H H.3985(34)
Saturday 'till Monday b (John H. Wagner)	Mr. Wix of Wickham (Darnley)	TBH 12 Nov 1904	FD & H H.3985(49)
Waiting for You b (John H. Wagner)	Mr. Wix of Wickham (Darnley)	TBH 12 Nov 1904	FD & H H.3985(58)
various other songs (see Bordman, pp. 35-36)	Mr. Wix of Wickham (Darnley)	unpublished	
How'd You Like to Spoon With Me? b,c (Edward Laska)	The Earl and The Girl (Caryll)	TBH 20 Mar 1905	FD & H H.3985(19)
The Chorus Girl, Two-Step b (instrumental)		TBH 8 May 1905	FD & H h.4120.ii(16)
The Frolic of a Breeze b (F. Clifford Harris; later P. G. Wodehouse & F. Clifford Harris)	The Beauty of Bath [London] (Haines)	TBH 20 Jul 1905	H & C H.3985(15)
Oh! Mr. Chamberlain, revised as Mr. Chamberlain c (Kern & P. G. Wodehouse)	The Beauty of Bath [London] (Haines)	TBH 20 Jul 1905	H & C H.3985(44)
Raining c (F. Clifford Harris)	The Catch of the Season (Haines)	TBH 20 Jul 1905	H & C H.3985(46)

Lettered notes begin on page 66.

* Publisher abbreviations: AH & C – Ascherberg, Hopwood & Crew; FD & H – Francis, Day & Hunter; H & C – Hopwood & Crew; JDK – Jerome D. Kern; TBH – T. B. Harms.

Copyright dates are taken, where available, from Library of Congress records, confirmed (with a few minor date variations) by British Library deposit dates. Where precise dates are not available from these sources, years of copyright have been obtained from printed copies in the collection of James J. Fuld of New York. Although printed copies were deposited for copyright as shown, in a few cases formal publication may not have taken place.

Song title and lyricist	Show and principal composer (U.S. prod'n unless stated)	Publisher and copyright date	U.K. copyright depositor & British Library shelf mark
The Bagpipe Serenade c (Kern)	The Rich Mr. Hoggenheimer (Englander)	TBH 20 Jul 1905	H & C H.3985(3)
Tulips (Two Lips) c (Kern)		TBH 20 Jul 1905	H & C H.3985(55)
Won't You Kiss Me Once Before You Go? c (Fred W. Leigh)	The Catch of the Season (Haines)	FD & H 24 Jul 1905	FD & H H.3985(62 & 63)
My Southern Belle (words Kern; music Max C. Eugene)	The Earl and The Girl (Caryll)	TBH 5 Sep 1905	H & C H.3983.kk(8)
Take Me On the Merry Go Round (Kern)	A Girl on the Stage [London] (Caryll)	TBH 11 Sep 1905	H & C H.3985(53)
An Autumn Bud (Kern[?])		TBH 25 Sep 1905	H & C not at British Library
Molly O'Hallerhan (Kern)	The Catch of the Season (Haines)	TBH 25 Sep 1905	H & C H.3985(39)
Farewell, Dear Toys, March (instrumental)	The Babes and The Baron (Haines)	TBH 14 Oct 1905	H & C h.4120.ii(17)
An Evening Hymn (with violin or flute obbligato) (Arthur Platt Howard)		TBH, for A. P. Howard 30 Dec 1905	H & C H.1187.ff(43)
Rosalie c (George Grossmith, Jr.)	The Spring Chicken [London] (Caryll & Monckton)	Chappell 1 Aug 1906	Chappell H.3985(48)

Song (Lyricist)	Show (Composer)	Date / Status	Catalog
Gwendoline of Grosvenor Square (George Grossmith, Jr.)	*The Spring Chicken* [London] (Caryll & Monckton)	unpublished	
Sunday Afternoon (George Grossmith, Jr.)	*The Spring Chicken* [London] (Caryll & Monckton)	unpublished	
The Leader of the Labour Party (George Grossmith, Jr.)	*Venus, 1906* [London] (Tippett)	unpublished	
Won't You Buy a Little Canoe? (George Grossmith, Jr.)	*Venus, 1906* [London] (Tippett)	unpublished	
Meet Me At Twilight [c] (F. Clifford Harris)	*The Little Cherub* (Caryll)	TBH 4 Aug 1906	AH & C H.3985(38)
Don't You Want a Paper, Dearie? [c,d] (Paul West)	*The Rich Mr. Hoggenheimer* (Englander)	TBH 3 Oct 1906	AH & C H.3985(11)
Poker Love (Card Duet) [d] (Paul West & Kern)	*The Rich Mr. Hoggenheimer* (Englander)	TBH 3 Oct 1906	AH & C H.3985(45)
All I Want Is You! (Paul West)	*My Lady's Maid* (Rubens)	TBH 8 Oct 1906	AH & C H.3985(1)
Blue, Blue! [a] (Paul West)		TBH 10 Nov 1906	AH & C H.3985(6)
My Hungarian Irish Girl (Paul West)		TBH 10 Dec 1906	AH & C H.3985(41)
A Plain Rustic Ride (words Kern; music Jackson Gouraud & Kern)	*The Little Cherub* (Caryll)	TBH 21 Jan 1907	AH & C H.3984.e(30)
A Recipe (Kern & Paul West)	*The Rich Mr. Hoggenheimer* (Englander)	TBH 15 Apr 1907	AH & C H.3985(47)

Song title and lyricist	Show and principal composer (U.S. prod'n unless stated)	Publisher and copyright date	U.K. copyright depositor & British Library shelf mark
I Just Couldn't Do Without You (Paul West)	*The White Chrysanthemum* (Talbot)	TBH 15 Apr 1907	AH & C H.3985(24)
Come Around on Our Veranda (Kern & Paul West)	*The Orchid* (Caryll & Monckton)	TBH 18 Apr 1907	AH & C H.3985(9)
Bill's a Liar (M. E. Rourke)		TBH 18 Apr 1907	AH & C H.3985(5)
I'm Well Known (Kern)		TBH 18 Apr 1907	AH & C H.3985(25)
The Subway Express c (James O'Dea)	*Fascinating Flora* (Kerker)	TBH 16 May 1907	AH & C H.3985(50)
Ballooning c (Paul West)	*Fascinating Flora* (Kerker)	TBH 20 May 1907	AH & C H.3985(4)
Katy Was a Business Girl (Paul West)	*Fascinating Flora* (Kerker)	TBH 20 May 1907	AH & C H.3985(30)
Right Now (words Kern; music Fred Fischer)	*Fascinating Flora* (Kerker)	TBH 20 May 1907	AH & C H.3983.pp(31)
I'd Like to Make a Smash Mit You (words Kern; music Fred Fischer)		TBH 25 May 1907	AH & C H.3983.pp(13)
The Little Church Around the Corner (M. E. Rourke)	*Fascinating Flora* (Kerker)	TBH 8 Jun 1907	AH & C H.3985(32)
Cheer Up, Girls! (M. E. Rourke)	*The Dairymaids* (Rubens & Tours)	TBH 19 Aug 1907	AH & C H.3985(8)
Little Eva (M. E. Rourke)	*The Dairymaids* (Rubens & Tours)	TBH 19 Aug 1907	AH & C H.3985(33)

Song	Show		
Under the Linden Tree (M. E. Rourke)	*The Little Cherub* (Caryll)	TBH 29 Aug 1907	AH & C H.3985(56)
I'd Like to Meet Your Father (M. E. Rourke)	*The Dairymaids* (Rubens & Tours)	TBH 14 Sep 1907	AH & C H.3985(22)
Eastern Moon (M. E. Rourke)	*The Morals of Marcus* (straight play)	TBH 4 Oct 1907	AH & C H.3985(13)
I've a Million Reasons (Why I Love You) (M. E. Rourke)	*The Dairymaids* (Rubens & Tours)	TBH 14 Oct 1907	AH & C H.3985(27)
Mary McGee (M. E. Rourke)	*The Dairymaids* (Rubens & Tours)	TBH 14 Oct 1907	AH & C H.3985(36)
Never Marry a Girl with Cold Feet (M. E. Rourke)	*The Dairymaids* (Rubens & Tours)	TBH 24 Oct 1907	AH & C H.3985(42)
Without the Girl — Inside! (M. E. Rourke & Kern)	*The Gay White Way* (Englander)	TBH 8 Nov 1907	AH & C H.3985(60)
I've a Little Favor (M. E. Rourke)	*The Rich Mr. Hoggenheimer* (Englander)	TBH 12 Nov 1907	AH & C H.3985(26)
Won't You Have a Little Feather? (Paul West)	*Peter Pan* (Crook)	TBH 6 Dec 1907	AH & C H.3985(61)
The Hay Ride [e] (M. E. Rourke)	*The Dairymaids* (Rubens & Tours)	TBH 20 Apr 1908	AH & C H.3985(17)
Aida McCluskie (C. H. Bovill)	*Fluffy Ruffles* (Francis)	TBH 12 Aug 1908	JDK F.1196.pp(3)
Take Care (C. H. Bovill)	*Fluffy Ruffles* (Francis)	TBH 12 Aug 1908	JDK F.1196.pp(2)
Meet Her With a Taximeter (C. H. Bovill)	*Fluffy Ruffles* (Francis)	TBH 12 Aug 1908	JDK H.3985(37)

Song title and lyricist	Show and principal composer (U.S. prod'n unless stated)	Publisher and copyright date	U.K. copyright depositor & British Library shelf mark
Mrs. Cockatoo (C. H. Bovill)		TBH 24 Aug 1908	JDK H.3985(40)
Nothing At All (M. E. Rourke)		TBH 24 Aug 1908	JDK H.3985(43)
Won't You Let Me Carry Your Parcel? (C. H. Bovill)	*Fluffy Ruffles* (Francis)	TBH 31 Aug 1908	JDK H.3985(64)
I Can't Say That You're the Only One (C. H. Bovill)	*The Girls of Gottenberg* (Caryll & Monckton)	TBH 12 Sep 1908	JDK H.3985(21)
Frieda (M. E. Rourke)	*The Girls of Gottenberg* (Caryll & Monckton)	TBH 14 Sep 1908	JDK H.3985(14)
Fräulein Katrina (George Grossmith, Jr.)	*The Girls of Gottenberg* (Caryll & Monckton)	unpublished	
Dining Out (George Grossmith, Jr.)	*Fluffy Ruffles* (Francis)	TBH 14 Sep 1908	JDK H.3985(10)
That's a Thing That's Really Wanted (?)	*Fluffy Ruffles* (Francis)	unpublished	
Steady Little Girlie (C. H. Bovill)	*Fluffy Ruffles* (Francis)	unpublished	
Sweetest Girl, Silly Boy, I Love You (Wallace Irwin)	*Fluffy Ruffles* (Francis)	TBH 15 Sep 1908	apparently not deposited in U.K.
There's Something Rather Odd About Augustus (C. H. Bovill)	*Fluffy Ruffles* (Francis)	TBH 17 Sep 1908	JDK H.3985(54)

The Gay Lothario [f] (C. H. Bovill)	A Waltz Dream [London] (Straus)	TBH 13 Oct 1908	JDK H.3985(16)
I'd Much Rather Stay At Home (C. H. Bovill)	A Waltz Dream (Straus)	TBH 13 Oct 1908	JDK H.3985(23)
Vienna (Adrian Ross)	A Waltz Dream (Straus)	TBH 13 Oct 1908	JDK H.3985(57)
If the Girl Wants You (M. E. Rourke)	Kitty Grey (Barratt & Talbot)	TBH & FD & H 19 Jan 1909	FD & H H.3985(28)
Just Good Friends (M. E. Rourke)	Kitty Grey (Barratt & Talbot)	TBH & FD & H 19 Jan 1909	FD & H H.3985(29)
Eulalie (M. E. Rourke)	Kitty Grey (Barratt & Talbot)	TBH & FD & H 1909	apparently not deposited in U.K.
A Boat Sails on Wednesday, Quartet (Adrian Ross & George Grossmith, Jr.)	The Dollar Princess (Fall)	TBH & FD & H 31 Aug 1909	AH & C H.3985(7)
Not Here! Not Here! (M. E. Rourke)	The Dollar Princess (Fall)	TBH & FD & H 31 Aug 1909	apparently not deposited in U.K.
Red, White and Blue (Adrian Ross)	The Dollar Princess (Fall)	TBH & FD & H 1909	apparently not deposited in U.K.
Suzette and Her Pet [g] (Percival Knight)	The Girl and the Wizard (Edwards)	Trebuhs 18 Sep 1909	FD & H H.3985(52)
By the Blue Lagoon (Percival Knight)	The Girl and the Wizard (Edwards)	TBH & FD & H 29 Sep 1909	apparently not deposited in U.K.
Frantzi (Percival Knight)	The Girl and the Wizard (Edwards)	TBH & FD & H 29 Sep 1909	apparently not deposited in U.K.
Howdy! How Do You Do? [h] (M. E. Rourke)	The Golden Widow (various composers)	TBH & FD & H 1909	apparently not deposited in U.K.

Song title and lyricist	Show and principal composer (U.S. prod'n unless stated)	Publisher and copyright date	U.K. copyright depositor & British Library shelf mark
Catamarang (Percival Knight)	*King of Cadonia* (Jones)	TBH & FD & H 31 Dec 1909	AH & C H.3985(31)
Come Along, Pretty Girl (M. E. Rourke)	*King of Cadonia* (Jones)	TBH & FD & H 31 Dec 1909	AH & C H.3985(31)
Every Girl I Meet (Percival Knight)	*King of Cadonia* (Jones)	TBH & FD & H 31 Dec 1909	AH & C H.3985(31)
Coo-oo, Coo-oo (Maurice Stonehill)	*King of Cadonia* (Jones)	TBH & FD & H 1 Jan 1910	AH & C uncatalogued vocal
The Blue Bulgarian Band (M. E. Rourke)	*King of Cadonia* (Jones)	TBH & FD & H 1910	apparently not deposited in U.K.
Hippopotamus (M. E. Rourke)	*King of Cadonia* (Jones)	TBH & FD & H 1910	apparently not deposited in U.K.
Lena, Lena (M. E. Rourke)	*King of Cadonia* (Jones)	TBH & FD & H 1910	apparently not deposited in U.K.
Mother and Father (M. E. Rourke)	*King of Cadonia* (Jones)	TBH & FD & H 1910	apparently not deposited in U.K.
Shine Out, All You Little Stars (M. E. Rourke)	*The Gay Hussars* (Kálmán)	TBH & FD & H 1910	apparently not deposited in U.K.
Whistle When You're Lonely (M. E. Rourke)	*The Echo* (Taylor)	TBH & FD & H 1 Sep 1910	FD & H uncatalogued vocal
Come, Tiny Goldfish to Me [i] (words Kern; music Harry Marlowe)	*Our Miss Gibbs* (Caryll & Monckton)	TBH & FD & H 1 Sep 1910	apparently not deposited in U.K.

I Don't Want You to be a Sister to Me [b] (Frederick Day)	*Our Miss Gibbs* (Caryll & Monckton)	TBH&FD&H 9 Sep 1910	FD & H uncatalogued vocal
Eight Little Girls (M. E. Rourke)	*Our Miss Gibbs* (Caryll & Monckton)	TBH&FD&H 29 Sep 1910	FD & H uncatalogued vocal
Betty's Advice [i] (Frederick Day)	*Our Miss Gibbs* (Caryll & Monckton)	unpublished(?)	
The Manicure Girl [j] (Frederick Day)	*The Hen Pecks* (Sloane)	TBH&FD&H 1910	apparently not deposited in U.K.

Notes on list of compositions

[a]Published editions bear dedications as follows: "In a Shady Bungalow" to Miss Minnie Haden; "Wine, Wine! (Champagne Song)" to Miss Ethel Prince; "Angling By a Babbling Brook" to Charles Lipson, Esq.; "Blue, Blue!" to E. W-H. [Edna Wallace Hopper].

[b]Besides the British Library copyright deposits, proof copies of the following are in the archives of Francis, Day & Hunter (now part of EMI Music Publishing): "Wine, Wine! (Champagne Song)," "Angling By a Babbling Brook," "Susan," "He'll Be There!," "The Downcast Eye," "My Celia," "McGuire Esquire," "Saturday 'till Monday," "Waiting for You," "How'd You Like to Spoon With Me?," "The Chorus Girl, Two-Step," "Frieda," "I Don't Want You to Be a Sister to Me."

[c]The following Kern songs of the period were published (or prepared for publication) by British publishers:

"McGuire Esquire" (additional verses by Fred W. Leigh) – Francis, Day & Hunter (plate no. F & D 8791), copyright 6 Jan 1905, British Library shelf mark H.3985(35).

"How'd You Like to Spoon With Me?" – Francis, Day & Hunter (plate no. F & D 8969), copyright 6 Jun 1905, British Library shelf mark H.3985(20); reissued as No. 258 of Francis, Day & Hunter's Sixpenny Popular Editions.

"Won't You Kiss Me Once Before You Go?" – Francis, Day & Hunter (plate no. F & D 9029), copyright 24 Jul 1905, British Library shelf mark H.3985(62/63).

"The Frolic of a Breeze" – deposited for copyright by Hopwood & Crew (plate no. H & C 4340) 20 Jul 1905, British Library shelf mark H.3985(15); published (by Ascherberg, Hopwood & Crew in 1906) only in piano-vocal score of *The Beauty of Bath*.

"Raining" – deposited for copyright by Hopwood & Crew (plate no. H & C 4341) 20 Jul 1905, British Library shelf mark H.3985(46); never published in U.K.

"The Bagpipe Serenade" – deposited for copyright by Hopwood & Crew (plate no. H & C 4342) 20 Jul 1905, British Library shelf mark H.3985(3); never published in U.K.

"Oh! Mr. Chamberlain" – deposited for copyright by Hopwood & Crew (plate
  no. H & C 4343) 20 Jul 1905, British Library shelf mark H.3985(44); published by
  Ascherberg, Hopwood & Crew as "Mr. Chamberlain" both separately (300 copies
  printed June 1906, 250 copies November 1906) and in piano-vocal score of *The
  Beauty of Bath*.

"Tulips (Two Lips)" – deposited for copyright by Hopwood & Crew (plate no.
  H & C 4344) 20 Jul 1905, British Library shelf mark H.3985(55); never published
  in U.K.

"Rosalie" – Chappell (plate no. 22831), copyright 1 Aug 1906, British Library
  shelf mark H.3985(48).

"Meet Me at Twilight" – Ascherberg, Hopwood & Crew (plate no. A H & C 4590;
  250 copies printed April 1907; 500 copies in shilling edition March 1908).

"Don't You Want a Paper, Dearie?" – Ascherberg, Hopwood & Crew (plate no.
  A H & C 4645; 500 copies printed August 1907).

"Ballooning" – Ascherberg, Hopwood & Crew (plate no. A H & C 4646; 500
  copies printed August 1907).

"Bakerloo (The Subway Express)" – Ascherberg, Hopwood & Crew (plate no.
  A H & C 4671; 500 copies printed October 1907).

[d]Copies of "Don't You Want a Paper, Dearie?" and "Poker Love" were only belatedly
deposited in the British Library on 26 Jan 1907.

[e]The British Library deposit copy of "The Hay Ride" shows the printed copyright
date manually altered from 1907 to 1908.

[f]"The Gay Lothario" was partially published in manuscript in *The Play Pictorial*,
number 69 (May 1908). [See illustration]

[g]Part of the melody of "Suzette and Her Pet" is by Georges Krier; hence the ownership of the
copyright by Trebuhs Publishing.

[h]The song "I Want You to See My Girl" in *The Golden Widow*, which Bordman suggests
may be by Kern, is actually by the British songwriters Harry Castling and Fred Godfrey.

68

[i] The music of "Come, Tiny Goldfish to Me" is copyright Monte Carlo Publishing Co., 1907.

[j] The lyrics of "Betty's Advice" ("Isn't It Nice to Have Somebody 'Crazy' About You?") and "The Manicure Girl" were published in Edward Montagu's *A Hundred and One Song Lyrics* (London: Francis, Day & Hunter, 1956).

APPENDIX 3: KERN'S BRITISH LYRICISTS (1905–10) . . .

Bovill, Charles Harry (1878–1918). Novelist and short story writer, he wrote lyrics for various musical comedies and revues, often to music by Philip Braham (1881–1934). He collaborated with Kern in 1908 on songs for *A Waltz Dream*, *The Girls of Gottenberg*, and *Fluffy Ruffles*. He died of wounds received in the First World War.

Day, Frederick (1878–1975). Son of one of the founders of Francis, Day & Hunter, he ran that firm's New York office from 1905 and collaborated with Kern on several songs before returning home in 1911. He also wrote lyrics under the pseudonym of Edward Montagu, under which name he published a collection of his lyrics in 1956. By that time he had become Chairman of Francis, Day & Hunter.

Grossmith, George (1874–1935). Known as George Grossmith, Jr., during the lifetime of his father, who created leading comic roles in the comic operas of Gilbert and Sullivan, he became a leading figure in the British musical theater as performer, book author, lyricist, and later producer. He was leading man at the Gaiety Theatre in its Edwardian heyday, appearing in all the major shows, including *The Orchid* (1903), *The Spring Chicken* (1905), *The Girls of Gottenberg* (1907), and *Our Miss Gibbs* (1909). He introduced many American songs to Britain and was lyricist and singer of Kern's contributions to *The Spring Chicken*. He was author of *Venus, 1906* and "The Gay Lothario" in *A Waltz Dream*, and appeared in New York in *Fluffy Ruffles*. Later he introduced to Britain "They Didn't Believe Me" in *To-Night's the Night* (London, 1915) and was producer of the London productions of the Kern shows *Theodore & Co.* (1916), *Oh, Boy!* (as *Oh, Joy!*, 1919), *Sally* (1921), *The Cabaret Girl* (1922), and *The Beauty Prize* (1923).

Harris, F. Clifford (*ca* 1875–1949). He wrote several lyrics for Kern in 1905–6 and later formed a highly successful partnership with the composer James W. Tate (1875–1922). With Tate he wrote "I Was a Good Little Girl Till I Met You" (1914), "A Broken Doll" (from *Samples*; 1916), "Ev'ry Little While" (from *Some*; 1916), "A Bachelor Gay" and "A Paradise for Two" (both from *The Maid of the Mountains*; 1917), and "Give Me a Little Cosy Corner" (1918).

Leigh, Fred W. (*d* 1924). For many years literary editor for Francis, Day & Hunter, he collaborated with Kern on "Won't You Kiss Me Once Before You Go?" He created many of the best-known British variety songs of the time, writing words and music of "Captain Gingah, O.T." and "Put On Your Tat-Ta, Little Girlie" and collaborating on "Don't Dilly Dally on the Way" (with Charles Collins), "The Galloping Major" (music by George Bastow), "Jolly Good Luck to the Girl Who Loves a Soldier" (music by Kenneth Lyle), "A Little of What You Fancy Does You Good" (with George Arthurs), and "Poor John!" and "Waiting at the Church" (both with music by Henry E. Pether [1867–1932]).

Ross, Adrian (really Arthur Reed Ropes [1859–1933]). Originally a Cambridge history don, he became a prolific lyricist for musical shows, including *The Merry Widow* (1907), *King of Cadonia* (1908), *The Dollar Princess* (1908), and *Our Miss Gibbs* (1909). He collaborated with Kern in 1908 and 1909 on songs for *A Waltz Dream* and *The Dollar Princess*.

Taylor, Charles Henry(*ca* 1860–1907). Playwright and lyricist, he contributed to many comic operas and musical comedies of the Edwardian era, including *The Catch of the Season* (1904) and Edward German's *Tom Jones* (1907). He provided the lyric for the theater version of Kern's "Won't You Kiss Me Once Before You Go?" and his 1902 lyric for "My Otaheite Lady" was adapted and reset by Kern for Pinero's *The Amazons* in 1913.

Wodehouse, Pelham Grenville (1881–1975). Celebrated author of humorous fiction, he provided the finished lyrics of Kern's contributions to *The Beauty of Bath* and later wrote lyrics for many New York and London shows, including several of Kern's. Best-known of these later song collaborations with Kern are "Till the Clouds Roll By" and "Bill." Curiously, he and Frederick Day, having survived Kern's other Edwardian British lyricists by over a quarter of a century, died within ten days of each other in February 1975.

. . . AND SOME EDWARDIAN BRITISH SHOW COMPOSERS (with whom Kern had contact, or for whose scores he composed interpolations)

Barratt, Augustus (*b* 1873). Composer of ballads and theater music, he composed *Kitty Grey* with Howard Talbot and later provided scores for C. B. Cochran revues, including *The Fun of the Fayre* (1921), which introduced to Britain Kern's "Whose Baby Are You?"

Caryll, Ivan (really Félix Tilkin [1861–1921]). Although he was born in Belgium and died in the U.S.A., this larger-than-life character spent the main part of his career in Britain. He conducted at the Gaiety Theatre in its musical comedy heyday and collaborated with Lionel Monckton on the scores for its shows, including *The Orchid* (1903), *The Spring Chicken* (1905), *The Girls of Gottenberg* (1907), and *Our Miss Gibbs* (1909). His many other British scores include *The Earl and the Girl* (1903) and *The Little Cherub* (1906), but he achieved his most lasting success after emigrating to the U.S.A., with the "Beautiful Lady" waltz in *The Pink Lady* (1911).

Crook, John (*ca* 1847–1922). A theater conductor and composer first in Manchester and later in London, he was for many years Frohman's musical director at the Duke of York's Theatre. As such he composed incidental music for *Peter Pan* (1904), *The "Mind the Paint" Girl* (1912), and *Rosy Rapture, the Pride of the Beauty Chorus* (1915), for all of which Kern contributed songs at various times. Crook's most successful individual composition was "The Coster's Serenade" for the Cockney comedian Albert Chevalier.

Darnley (really McCarthy), **Herbert** (1871–1947). Comedian, dramatist, and songwriter, he provided many musical sketches for the variety performer Dan Leno, including "The Beefeater" ("The Tower of London"), and the musical comedy *Mr. Wix of Wickham*. In the latter, Leno made a highly successful tour, and for its American adaptation Kern provided several songs. Darnley also wrote material for Fred Karno.

Finck (really van de Vinck), **Herman** (1872–1939). Son of a Dutch immigrant theater musician, he was conductor at London's Palace Theatre for many years. As such he orchestrated and conducted some of Kern's early song successes, including "How'd You Like to Spoon With Me?" in 1906, "You're Here and I'm Here" in 1914, and "Some Sort of Somebody" in 1916. He later conducted the London production of *Show Boat* at the Theatre Royal, Drury Lane. His own most successful compositions were written for the Palace Theatre: the dance "In the Shadows" (1910) and the songs "Gilbert the Filbert" and "I'll Make a Man of You" (both from *The Passing Show*; 1914).

Haines, Herbert Edgar (1879–1923). Son of a Manchester theater conductor, he conducted at various London theaters and was principal composer of the series of Seymour Hicks musicals *The Catch of the Season* (1904), *The Talk of the Town* (1905), *The Beauty of Bath* (1906), and *My Darling* (1907). He later composed and conducted music to accompany silent films as well as much light orchestral music, of which the best-known is the "triumphant march" "The London Scottish" (1916).

Jones, Guy (1875–1959). Younger brother of Sidney, he too was a theater conductor, composer, and arranger, active particularly in Birmingham. He composed the score for the Seymour Hicks musical *The Gay Gordons* (1907).

Jones, Sidney (1861–1946). Son of a military bandmaster and theater conductor, he was for many years a conductor of comic opera and musical comedy. He achieved success as a composer with the song "Linger Longer Loo" for the burlesque *Don Juan* (1893) and went on to provide the scores for a series of George Edwardes musical plays at Daly's Theatre, of which *The Geisha* (1896) achieved success around the globe. However, his musical style was rooted in the nineteenth century, and after 1900 he felt increasingly out of touch with developments in the musical theater. *King of Cadonia* (1908) was the most successful of his later scores, and he also composed part of *The Girl from Utah* (1914) for whose American version Kern wrote "They Didn't Believe Me."

Monckton, Lionel (1861–1924). Probably the most fluent melodist Britain ever produced, he contributed to most of the major successes of the musical theater during the Edwardian era. He was the principal composer of *A Country Girl* (1902) and *The Quaker Girl* (1910), as well as of *The Cingalee* (1904), whose setting may have been a source of inspiration for Kern's *Lucky* (1927). He collaborated with Ivan Caryll on the scores for Gaiety Theatre successes, including *The Orchid* (1903), *The Spring Chicken* (1905), *The Girls of Gottenberg* (1907), and *Our Miss Gibbs* (1909), and with Howard Talbot on *The Arcadians* (1909). His lilting melodies also graced many other scores of the era as "additional numbers."

Rubens, Paul Alfred (1875–1917). After Monckton he was the most gifted melodist of the era, and was able to combine this gift with a deeper sense of emotion and a good sense of theatrical effect. He was versatile enough to write book, lyrics, and music for several shows, including his masterpiece, *Miss Hook of Holland* (1907), which enjoyed considerable international success. His other shows included *Lady Madcap* (1904; became in the U.S.A. *My Lady's Maid*), *The Dairymaids* (with Frank E. Tours; 1906), *The Sunshine Girl* (1912), and *To-Night's the Night* (1914). In addition, his "comedy with music" *Mr. Popple (of Ippleton)* (1905) was revised and provided with new songs by Kern to become the first of the Princess Theatre musicals, *Nobody Home*. Like Monckton, Rubens provided many additional numbers for other composers' scores. He was troubled by ill-health throughout his short life.

Slaughter, Walter (1860–1908). Composer of ballads and theater music, he was conductor at many London theaters, including the Coliseum up to the time of his death.

His many scores for pantomime, burlesque, musical comedy, and comic opera included music for the stage adaptation of *Alice in Wonderland* (1886), for the successful Seymour Hicks children's show *Bluebell in Fairyland* (1901), and for *An English Daisy* (Reading, 1902), for whose American version Kern provided additional numbers.

Stuart, Leslie (really Thomas Augustine Barrett [1864–1928]). Composer and lyricist of such British song classics as "Soldiers of the Queen" (1895), "Little Dolly Daydream" (1897), and "Lily of Laguna" (1898), he repeated their success with his first musical comedy score, *Florodora* (1899). After *The Silver Slipper* (1901) and *The Belle of Mayfair* (1905), however, he faded from prominence. He suffered particularly from the activities of pirate music publishers, and after vainly trying his luck in the U.S.A. he returned to Britain and died in poverty. His brother, Lester Barrett, was a music-hall singer and lyricist of many songs including "I Used to Sigh for the Silvery Moon" (music by Herman Darewski; 1909).

Talbot (really Munkittrick), **Howard** (1865–1928). American-born but English-bred, he was technically perhaps the most accomplished of all the Edwardian theater composers. He enjoyed success with his scores for *A Chinese Honeymoon* (1899) and *The White Chrysanthemum* (1905) and collaborated with Augustus Barratt on *Kitty Grey* (1901), but did his best work in partnership with the more fluent melodists Monckton and Rubens. With Monckton he composed the classic *The Arcadians* (1909), which included his own most popular number, the lugubrious "My Motter." He was also highly regarded as a theater conductor.

Tippett, Constance. Of American origin, she was briefly active in the London popular musical theater around the time of Kern's early visits. She was composer and arranger of the score for the Empire Theatre revue *Venus, 1906*, to which Kern contributed.

Tours, Frank Edward (1877–1963). Son of the Dutch immigrant musician Berthold Tours, he achieved early success with his setting of Kipling's "Mother o' Mine" (1903). He conducted and contributed additional numbers to many Edwardian musical comedies, collaborated with Rubens on *The Dairymaids* (1906), and composed the score of *The Dashing Little Duke* (1909) for Seymour Hicks. He then went to America, collaborated with Kern on *La Belle Paree* (1911), and subsequently pursued a varied career in the theater and cinema on both sides of the Atlantic. He remained closely associated with Kern, and according to B. C. Hilliam's *Flotsam's Follies* (London: Arthur Barron, 1948, pp. 56–57) the two used to play a correspondence word-game. The idea was to turn one word into another with the fewest possible letter changes. Thus when Tours, previously a confirmed bachelor, surprised his friends by getting married, he received from Kern the message, "What about turning Tours into Pater in nine?"

APPENDIX 4: SUMMARY OF KERN'S EDWARDIAN LONDON VISITS

1905 (spring/summer) - Probable first visit to London

    - Songwriting collaborations with Fred W. Leigh and F. Clifford Harris

    - Songwriting agreement with Charles Frohman

    - Transfer of Harms agency from Francis, Day & Hunter to Hopwood & Crew

    - (June 24) Francis, Day & Hunter outing to Box Hill

1906 (winter/spring) - Living in Jermyn Street

    - Member of Walsingham Club

    - Collaborations with George Grossmith

    - (January) Night drive to High Wycombe

    - (February 12) First night of "How'd You Like to Spoon With Me?" at Palace Theatre

    - (March) Meeting and collaboration with P. G. Wodehouse

    - (March 19) First night of *The Beauty of Bath* at Aldwych Theatre

    - (March 22) First night of "new edition" of *The Spring Chicken* at Gaiety Theatre

    - (April 17) First night of *Venus, 1906* at Empire Theatre

    - (May 5) First night of *A Girl on the Stage* at Prince of Wales' Theatre

1908 (winter/spring)	- Collaborations with C. H. Bovill, Adrian Ross, and George Grossmith on *A Waltz Dream*, *Fluffy Ruffles*, and *The Girls of Gottenberg*
	- (March 7) First night of *A Waltz Dream* at Hicks Theatre
	- (May 5) First night of revival of *The Dairymaids* at Queen's Theatre
1909 (spring/summer)	- Collaborations with Adrian Ross and George Grossmith on *The Dollar Princess*
	- Courting Eva Leale
	- (April 29) Julia Sanderson in *The Dashing Little Duke* at Hicks Theatre
1910 (fall)	- (October 25) Marriage to Eva Leale at Walton-on-Thames

INDEX

84

Andrew Lamb is well known to an international readership as a specialist in "light music" (as his compatriots in England call it). Since the mid-1960's he has written for such journals as *The Musical Times*, *Opera*, *Gramophone*, *Music & Letters*, and *American Music* on popular song, operetta, *opéra-comique*, and American musical theater. More than 130 articles in these fields appear over his signature in *The New Grove Dictionary of Music and Musicians*, and he has written many others for the forthcoming *New Grove Dictionary of American Music*—including the one on Jerome Kern. The present monograph is one of several contributions he has made on behalf of Jerome Kern in the composer's centennial year.

The Institute for Studies in American Music at Brooklyn College, City University of New York, is a division of the College's Conservatory of Music. It was established in 1971. The Institute contributes to American-music studies in several ways. It publishes a series of monographs, a periodical newsletter, and special publications of various kinds. It serves as an information center and sponsors conferences and symposia dealing with all areas of American music including art music, popular music, and the music of oral tradition. The Institute also encourages and supports research by offering fellowships to distinguished scholars and, for assistance in funded projects, to junior scholars as well. The Institute supervises the series of music editions *Recent Researches in American Music* (published by A–R Editions, Inc.) and is the administrative seat of the Charles Ives Society. I.S.A.M. activities also include presentation of concerts and lectures at Brooklyn College for students, faculty, and the public.